# The Heart of the Bible

## RETOLD FOR CHILDREN

Over 100 key passages for teachers,
parents and children's workers
to read aloud

# Patricia Ainge

www.kevinmayhew.com

For Chris, who brought such a lot of love,
light and laughter into our lives.

 KM PUBLISHING

First published in Great Britain in 2014 by Kevin Mayhew Ltd
Buxhall, Stowmarket, Suffolk IP14 3BW
Tel: +44 (0) 1449 737978  Fax: +44 (0) 1449 737834
E-mail: info@kevinmayhew.com

www.kevinmayhew.com

ISBN 978 1 84867 703 6
Catalogue No. 1501429

Cover design by Rob Mortonson
© Images used under licence from Shutterstock Inc.
Edited by Linda Ottewell
Typeset by Richard Weaver

Printed and bound in Great Britain

# Contents

# The New Testament

# About the author

Married, with three children and four grandsons of her own, Patricia Ainge has worked in Catholic schools for over twenty years, which has given her a great deal of experience with children. Religious education has been a key part of her role throughout her teaching career. She is currently Deputy Head at English Martyrs Catholic Primary School in Wakefield.

Patricia has an extensive background in liturgy, working both in schools, in her parish and in the Diocese of Leeds. She has been a member of the Diocesan Council for Liturgy and the Council of Laity and has taken on different roles at different times within her own parish, including being part of the liturgy group and sacramental preparation. She has a particular interest and expertise in liturgical dance, working with both adults and children to enhance prayer and liturgy.

# Introduction

## The background to this book

Those of us who seek to pass on our faith to our children want it to be something that is real and alive for them. We want it to be something that speaks to them as children of the twenty-first century; something that has a meaning and significance for them; something that shapes their lives.

It was this motivation that led to my writing *The Heart of the Bible, Retold for Children*. I wanted a version of the Bible that spoke to children not just as a text that ought to be read, but as a story – a story that spoke to them about a set of living, breathing people who lived many years ago and whose story is now their story.

To achieve this I needed to do three things. Firstly, the language needed to be simpler than a traditional Bible – it needed to be readable for children of primary school age so that older ones could pick up the book and read it for themselves and younger children could have the book read to them and be able to understand and identify with the people in the stories.

The second thing I needed to do was to be selective about the content. Most of us do not expect our young children to be conversant with the whole of the text of the Bible. Indeed few adults are – so I had to choose the stories that were the most read and also that children would understand and identify with.

Finally, I needed to use a little imaginative freedom in their retelling so that the characters would to some extent become real to the children reading them and would engage their interest. Nothing added has altered the significance or essential meaning of the story – it has merely made the characters act and react as people would.

In this way I hoped to create a heart of the Bible for primary school aged children which would be accessible and readable as well as enjoyable and memorable for them.

## Who is this book for?

The book is useful to many different groups of people. Firstly, it is written for anybody who is engaged in teaching children the stories of their faith. This includes a great many different people. One key group is parents; parents who want their children to have a set of Bible stories that they can read or have read to them at any time. My children, when young, would often read their children's Bible during church services that they could not understand. Other people may choose to read them as stories.

Another key group are primary school teachers. All schools that follow the National Curriculum have statutory guidance to follow for Religious Education. The content taught in primary schools, whether state or denominational, all include Christianity and all have an element of Scripture. Children need to know the stories from the Bible in order to progress.

In Catholic primary schools the levels of attainment set by the Bishops of England and Wales demand that the children should have a good knowledge of Bible stories, both Old and New Testament, if they are to progress through the levels expected. A Bible that offers this to the children in child-friendly language is invaluable.

A third group for whom the book would be suitable is any church group that needs the Word of God for children, e.g. Sunday schools, children's worship etc.

So the book is aimed at any group or individual who needs to enable access to Scripture for children. Most of these groups do not need access to the full Bible and therefore a set of well-chosen extracts from the Bible is ideal. The fact that the children can access these themselves is also highly desirable.

Secondly, the book is useful for people who plan and lead collective worship of any form for children. As well as lessons and personal reading, the book can be used in children's collective worship, liturgies, prayer times and assemblies. A range of Scripture which children can respond to in different ways is needed when leading worship and access to simple Old and New Testament readings and psalms enriches opportunities for collective prayer with children.

## Which stories have been chosen? What is the chronology?

The book mostly follows the pattern of an adult Bible. It is divided into the Old and New Testaments and each section has an introduction that explains its part in the full Bible. The story of God's people, which is the first section, gives a picture of the story of the people of God from the creation of the world to the story of Jonah. This is then followed by a selection of psalms. This section is very useful for creative work with children as well as worship and prayer time.

The final section in the Old Testament is the Prophets. While many of the sayings of the prophets are too difficult for children, it would be wrong to omit them altogether from a book entitled *The Heart of the Bible*. It is almost impossible to put them into their full context and so a short introduction has been included which explains what the prophets did and that these are only selected sayings.

The extracts chosen are a selection of some of the sayings which children might come across as they journey through their primary years. The poetry of the sayings has a value of its own and means that they can be used in many different ways in schools and church groups.

The New Testament was harder to create a chronology for as the Gospels do not always feature stories in the same order, e.g. the cleansing of the Temple is in Holy Week in the synoptic Gospels and is nearer the beginning of the ministry of Jesus in John. With the audience and purpose of the book in mind I decided to pursue the following course.

I would follow the obvious chronology of the life of Jesus from birth to death and then resurrection.

For the years of his ministry, however, I decided to collect events together in a topical way. I did this for several reasons:

1. It is less important for children to know the actual order of the stories than the content.

2. It seemed that children would remember stories that had a similar focus if they were grouped together.

3. In schools it is often important for the children to be able to refer to several aspects of Jesus' life to support their work, e.g. several miracles etc. For this reason it seemed that grouping them as I have made sense.

These reasons together outweighed any drawbacks in collecting events and stories under their topics rather than trying to create a timeline for the life of Jesus.

The final section of the book is gathered under the title *The Early Church* as it tells the story of the difficulties and joys of being the people who began the Christian Church.

# The Old Testament

What happened before Jesus was born

# The story of God's people

This section tells the different stories of God's people and some of the things that they did.

## The beginning of the world: the story of God's creation

At the very beginning of time there was darkness. Only God's Spirit was there. So God said, 'Let there be light.' And light appeared. God looked at this and saw that the light was good and so day and night began. Next God decided that the sky and the earth should be separated and so it was. God looked at this and saw that was good too. Then he thought it would be good to have the dry land separate from the water. He called the dry land earth and the water he called seas and oceans.

But everything looked very bare and empty so he decided that he needed something that was alive. He thought for a while and then, out of his imagination came grass and trees and all different kinds of plants.

He was really pleased with his world but he still hadn't finished because he wanted to make it even better. He decided that maybe something to shine in the sky so that day would follow night would be a good idea. He created a huge light called the sun for the day and smaller lights called the moon and stars for night.

Now God was even more pleased with what he had done but he saw that the earth and the seas still looked empty and he decided to create living things that could move about in his new world. Now God had a marvellous imagination so he didn't just create one kind of creature, he created lots and lots of different ones. Some of them had legs and could run on the earth; some of them had fins and could swim in the sea, some of them had wings so they could fly in the air. He imagined all sorts of creatures, from elephants with long trunks, giraffes with long necks and tiny little insects that scuttled along the ground. He loved colour and so he made them all different colours. The world was looking better and better.

God looked at everything he had created and was really happy but he still felt as though something was missing.

'There's nobody to look after my new world,' he said to himself. And then he had another idea. 'I know what I'll do,' he said to himself. 'I'll make people in my own image and they can take care of my world.' So he created people and he blessed them and he said to them, 'Go and enjoy my beautiful world. Look after it for me and take care of all of the living things that I have created.'

And when he looked at his world that day he was delighted. 'I've done an excellent job,' he said to himself. 'Now it's time for a rest!'

# The story of Adam and Eve

God created a garden in a place called Eden and he put the people he had created there. The man he called Adam and the woman he called Eve. He asked them to look after everything he had created; to name all of the creatures and to tend everything that grew. He told them that they could eat any of the food that grew in the garden – all except for the fruit that grew from one special tree. This was a tree that was called the Tree of Knowledge.

For a long time they did exactly as God had asked. They named all of the creatures and they tended the plants and things that grew. They ate the food that grew in the garden but they did not touch the fruit that grew on the Tree of Knowledge.

One day, though, that changed. Eve was near the Tree of Knowledge when she heard a soft, hissing voice behind her.

'Why don't you try the fruit?' said the voice.

Eve turned quickly and saw a snake.

'I must not,' she answered hurriedly. 'The Lord lets us eat any of the other fruit but not this one.'

'Why not?' said the tempting voice. 'Why shouldn't you eat this one?'

'I think it might be bad for us,' faltered Eve.

The snake swayed from side to side, shaking its head. 'Oh no,' it hissed gently. 'The only reason that God does not want you to eat this fruit is because it will give you knowledge. You will know as much as God does.'

Eve stared at the snake. The fruit looked delicious, ripe and juicy.

'Oh no,' she said. 'Surely that can't be true. I'm sure it will be bad for us.'

But the snake could hear the weakness in her voice.

'Oh yes, it is true,' he persisted. 'You will be wise and know everything.'

He watched her and saw that she was tempted.

'Just a little bite,' the snake's silky voice said. 'You only need to take a little bite.'

Eve could not resist the temptation. She stretched out her arm and in a moment one of the fruits was in her hand. Lifting it to her mouth she took a quick bite.

Half-excited, half-guilty she called to Adam.

'What have you done?' he asked, horrified. 'You know we shouldn't eat that fruit.'

'But it's delicious,' said Eve. 'It will teach us everything that God knows. Come on, quickly, try some.'

So Adam took the fruit from Eve and took a bite.

Just then they heard the Lord walking in the garden. Horrified at what they had done, they rushed into the trees to hide.

'Come out,' said God. 'Why are you hiding from me?'

And God knew what they had done. They had disobeyed him.

And so God sent Adam and Eve out of the garden. He told them that from now on they would have to make a living for themselves from the land and that things would be very difficult for them. They would have to work hard all of their lives and they would know what it was like to feel pain.

So Adam and Eve left the garden and were never allowed back.

# The story of Noah

Many years after God had created the world, there lived a man whose name was Noah. He lived with his wife and three sons, whose names were Shem, Ham and Japheth.

Now Noah was a good man but there were many, many people living then who were not good at all. So one day God said to Noah,

'I need to do something about the number of wicked people but I do not want any harm to come to you. You must do what I say. Build an ark and take on board your family and all of the different animals. You must take two of each kind because there will be a great flood and I want you to be safe.'

Noah did exactly as God asked. He built the ark and took on board his family and two of every kind of living creature.

Soon the sky grew dark and it began to rain. It rained and rained for forty days and forty nights and the ark rose as the waters rose and it floated on the surface, keeping Noah and his family safe.

The waters rose higher and higher until the whole of the land was covered, from the lowest valley to the highest mountain peak.

After forty days it stopped raining but the waters remained high. They covered all of the land for one hundred and fifty days. And Noah waited, safe in the ark.

And then, after one hundred and fifty days, God sent a wind across the earth and the waters began to drain away. Little by little the waters went down until the ark came to rest on a mountain whose name was Ararat.

Still Noah waited, safe in the ark, until he could see the land. Then he opened the window and sent out one of the doves but the dove could not find any dry land to perch on and so it came back to the ark.

Noah waited a little longer and the waters still went down, bit by bit. When he thought it was time, he sent the dove out again. This time it came back with an olive leaf that was fresh and Noah knew that the water must have fallen below the treetops. Seven days later he sent out the dove again and this time the dove did not return. Noah knew that it must have found somewhere to nest so he waited no longer. He left the ark with all of his family and all of the animals and they began a new life.

Then God said to Noah, 'I will make a promise to you and all the people who come after you. There shall be no flood to destroy the earth again. See, here is the sign of my promise. I will put a rainbow in the sky and it will be a sign of the promise between me and you.'

So Noah and his family started a new life, knowing that God would never again cover the earth with water.

# The story of Abraham

Many, many years after Noah had died, one of the women in his family had a son called Abram. When Abram grew up he married a woman called Sarai. They were very happy together except for one thing. They had no children. Now God knew that Abram, like Noah, was a very special person and he chose him to do a very special job. One day he spoke to Abram and this is what he said:

'Abram, I want you to leave your country and the people you know and go to a country I will show you. I will make you a great nation. I will bless you and make your name famous. You are going to be a blessing.'

So Abram did as God asked and went with Sarai and his nephew who was called Lot and all the people who followed them and went to the land of Canaan. He travelled around to different places but always tried to be ready to listen for God's voice.

Some years later God spoke to Abram in a vision and made a promise to him:

'Do not be afraid, Abram. I will protect you and give you a great reward.'

But this time Abram replied, 'Lord Yahweh, what is the point of your gifts when I have no children to follow me to pass on the gifts and everything that I own?'

So God replied, 'You will have a child and your family will grow and continue for many years. Look at the stars in the sky. That is how many descendants you will have.'

Abram could hardly believe what he was hearing but God told him to make a sacrifice of different animals so Abram did as God asked. Then God spoke again.

'Your descendants, though, will live in a land that is not their own for a long time and they will be slaves for many hundreds of years but do not worry, for one day they will be freed and they will own things of their own. Then I will punish the nation that has made them slaves.'

And when the sun had set, a smoking fire pot and a flaming torch appeared and God made an agreement with Abram.

'I will give this country from the river of Egypt to the Great River – the River Euphrates – to your descendants.'

Years passed and still Abram had no children. He began to think that God had forgotten him but one day God spoke to him again. Abram listened in wonder as God repeated his promise.

'I will give the land of Canaan to you and to your descendants. I will be your God and you will be my people.'

This time, though, God gave him another instruction.

'You must change your name from Abram to Abraham and you must change your wife's name from Sarai to Sarah and she will bear you a son and you will name him Isaac.'

And what God had promised came true and Sarah had a son. Abraham and Sarah were full of joy and they called him Isaac.

## Abraham is tested

When Isaac, Abraham's son, was growing up, God tested Abraham. He spoke to Abraham and said, 'I want you to give me your son Isaac. Take him to the land of Moriah and offer him to me as a sacrifice on the mountain there.'

Abraham was horrified. Isaac was his son and he loved him but he knew that he had to obey God. So Abraham, although heavy-hearted, set off to do what God asked. He told Isaac to come with him because they were going to make a sacrifice to God as was their custom.

They reached the place and Isaac said, 'Father, I can see the wood and the fire but I cannot see the lamb for the sacrifice.'

And Abraham, his heart full of sadness, replied, 'God will provide the lamb.'

And so he prepared to sacrifice his son but – just as he was going to do so – a voice spoke and said,

'No, Abraham, do not sacrifice your son. Now God knows how much you love and fear him and he will reward you for your obedience. Your descendants will be as many as the stars in the sky and the grains of sand on the seashore.'

# The story of Isaac's family

When Abraham was an old man, Isaac married a girl named Rebekah. She had twin sons whom they named Esau and Jacob. Now Esau, who was born first, grew to be a skilled hunter. He was the elder son and so would follow Isaac as the head of the family when Isaac died. This was his birthright. Jacob, who was born second, grew up to be a quiet man who stayed around the home.

One day, Esau returned from hunting. Jacob was at home, making a stew. Esau said to him,

'Give me some of that stew, brother, for I am so hungry.'

Jacob replied, 'I'll give you some but it has to be in return for your birthright as the eldest.'

Esau, who was exhausted, answered, 'I don't care about my birthright; just let me eat.'

So Jacob gave him the stew and he gave Jacob his birthright. Now he would be head of the family when Isaac died.

# The story of Joseph

Jacob married and had twelve sons. The youngest of the sons were called Joseph and Benjamin. Now Jacob loved Joseph more than any of his other sons and this made his older brothers jealous. Jacob had a special coat made for Joseph out of many different-coloured cloths.

## Joseph's dreams

One day Joseph came to his brothers and told them that he had had a dream.

'I dreamed that we were tying the sheaves of corn in the field and suddenly the sheaf that was mine rose up and stood upright. Then all of your sheaves bowed down to mine.'

But his brothers were angry with Joseph. They did not like the idea that he was better than they were.

Another day he told them that he had had a different dream. This time he had seen the sun and the moon and eleven stars all bowing down to him but his brothers, instead of listening to him, got even more angry and decided among themselves that they needed to get rid of Joseph.

## Joseph's brothers are angry with him

Their chance came one day when they had gone out into the fields to tend their sheep. Jacob sent Joseph out after them to see if everything was all right. But as soon as they saw Joseph coming they said to each other,

'Look, here's Joseph. Let's kill him now and leave him here and then we will be rid of him and his dreams.'

But Reuben, the eldest, said, 'We should not kill him because his blood will be on our hands. Let's throw him into this pit and the wild animals will come and kill him.'

So when Joseph reached them, they seized him and tore off his coat of many different colours and threw him into the pit.

## Joseph is sold as a slave

The brothers sat down to eat a meal when they noticed a group of Ishmaelites coming along and Judah, one of the brothers, said to the others,

'Why do we need to kill Joseph at all? After all, he is our brother. Let's sell him to these Ishmaelites instead.'

And so that is what they did and Joseph was taken away as a slave into Egypt.

Meanwhile the brothers killed a goat and dipped Joseph's coat into the blood. Then they took the coat and went home where they told their father, Jacob, that they had found this coat in the wilderness.

'It is Joseph's,' said Jacob, trembling. 'He must have been killed by a wild animal.'

And Jacob was heartbroken at the loss of his son and mourned him for many days.

When Joseph arrived in Egypt he was bought by a captain of the guards named Potiphar and for many years he served Potiphar well. Potiphar was pleased with his service and relied on him more and more. One day though, that all changed.

Potiphar's wife was bored and she wanted Joseph to spend more time with her but every time Joseph, who was loyal to Potiphar, refused. Eventually Potiphar's wife was angry and she pretended that Joseph had offended her and he was thrown into prison.

## Joseph explains the prisoners' dreams

Even in prison Joseph was kind. He looked after many prisoners and people started to treat him with respect. Two of the men who were in prison with him worked for the Pharaoh, who was king of Egypt. They both had dreams that they did not understand. They described their dreams to Joseph and he offered to tell them what he thought they meant.

The first was the chief butler. His dream had shown a vine with three branches. Grapes had appeared on all of these branches and then the butler had dreamed that he had pressed the grapes and poured the juice into the Pharaoh's cup. He had given the cup to Pharaoh.

Joseph listened to what the man had to say. He thought for a moment and then he said, 'Listen carefully because this is what your dream means. In three days you will be free again and you will go back to your old job and the Pharaoh will accept you. When you do, please tell him about me because I have been stolen away from my own land and want to go back to my Father.'

The butler was overjoyed. 'If only you're right,' he said.

The second man to dream was the chief baker for the Pharaoh. He too told Joseph his dream hoping for a happy ending.

'Tell me your dream,' invited Joseph.

'I had three baskets on my head and in one of them were three white loaves of bread – but then the birds came and ate the bread out of the basket.'

He looked hopefully at Joseph but Joseph felt a great sadness descending on him because he knew that the dream did not have a happy message.

He looked at the baker and then said, 'The three baskets mean three days but the Pharaoh will not find you innocent. Your dream means that in three days you will be found guilty.'

Everything that Joseph had foretold came true; the baker was killed but the butler went free. He forgot his promise to Joseph though and never told the Pharaoh about his request.

## Joseph explains the Pharaoh's dreams

Two years later the Pharaoh himself had a very disturbing dream. He dreamed that he was standing by the river when seven fat and healthy cows came out of the river and stood on the bank. Then seven very thin and hungry-looking cows came out, stood by the fat cows and ate them up. He woke up feeling very uneasy.

Later he had another dream where one plump stalk held seven heads of grain. Just then seven thin heads of grain came up and greedily ate up the seven plump grains.

Pharaoh was very worried. Nobody seemed to be able to tell him the meaning of his dreams but he knew that they were very important. Just then the butler stepped forward.

'I have remembered that when I was in prison I had a disturbing dream and there was a young Hebrew man who interpreted this dream for me and what he said came true.'

So Pharaoh sent for Joseph and asked him if he would tell him what his dreams meant.

'God will give me an answer,' said Joseph.

So Pharaoh told Joseph about his dreams and Joseph thought for a while and then answered.

'The seven fat cows and the seven fat ears of grain mean that there will be seven years in Egypt where the harvests are good and there is plenty of food. The seven thin cows and the seven thin ears of grain, however, mean that these seven years of plenty will be followed by seven years of famine where there will be very little food for anybody in Egypt.

What you need to do is to prepare for this. Choose a wise man who will organise things for you so that, during the years of plenty, you store up lots of food that you will be able to use when the years of famine come.'

## Joseph becomes a leader

The Pharaoh was so impressed that he chose Joseph to be this man who would lead them through the famine. 'You have shown me how wise you can be,' he said. 'I think you are the best man to lead us in this crisis.'

It happened just as Joseph had said and for seven years there was good weather and a rich harvest with grain for everybody and plenty left over. Joseph stored this grain and soon Egypt had enough grain to last them for years. It was just as well they had because after seven years were up, the weather became much worse and the harvest failed. There would have been a famine in the land if it hadn't have been for Joseph's careful planning and storing of grain in the good years. As it was, there was still plenty for everybody.

The poor harvest, however, was not just in Egypt and soon people who lived in other lands began to starve. They heard about Joseph and how Egypt had plenty of food and so they sent messengers to beg him to sell them some grain and Joseph agreed.

## Joseph's family come to buy food

Jacob and his sons soon began to starve as there was no grain in their land and so Jacob sent his sons to Egypt to beg them to sell them some food. They set off and, arriving in Egypt, came before Joseph to ask for food. They had no idea that the person they were asking was Joseph. They thought Joseph was a slave somewhere and did not know about his good fortune and clever management. Joseph, however, recognised his brothers and made a plan.

## Joseph's plan

Joseph pretended that he thought that they were spies from another land and however much the brothers told him they were not, he refused to believe them.

'We swear we are not spies,' pleaded the brothers. 'We are the sons of Jacob and we only need to buy food. We have money to give you in exchange.'

Joseph pretended to consider this. Finally he said,

'I know you said you have a younger brother. Bring him here to me and I will believe your story.'

And he threw them all into prison.

Three days passed and then Joseph pretended to change his mind.

'I have decided that you might be honest men,' he said. 'I will keep one of you in prison and I will give the rest of you the grain you ask for. You must bring your youngest brother to me if you want me to release the brother that I am keeping in prison.'

The brothers agreed to this and Simeon offered to stay. Then Joseph had sacks filled with grain and sent them off. What they did not know was that he had not taken their money but had put the bags with the coins in them back into the sacks with the grain. It did not take them long to realise that Joseph had given them the grain free and they could not understand it. They hurried home to Jacob.

'The man who is lord of the country thought we were spies,' they said. And they told him everything that had happened.

'We must take Benjamin,' they said.

But Jacob said no. 'I have lost your brother Joseph,' he said. 'I have now lost Simeon. I cannot also lose Benjamin.'

So they stayed at home but soon the grain was eaten.

'You will have to go back and ask for more,' said Jacob.

'But we cannot,' said the brothers. 'The lord will not see us unless we take Benjamin with us.'

Finally Jacob agreed. 'Take gifts and extra money,' he said, 'and maybe this lord will release your brother Simeon and will also send back Benjamin.'

They set off once again and arrived in Egypt. Once again Joseph received them and released Simeon. Joseph was overjoyed to see Benjamin but he did not show this. Instead he gave them food and drink and let them rest. The next day he had their sacks filled with grain but he told his steward to place his silver cup into Benjamin's sack. Then he said goodbye to them and they set off on their way.

## Joseph tricks his brothers

Joseph let his brothers travel a little way and then he sent his servants after them.

'Stop!' they cried. 'My master has lost a silver cup and he thinks that one of you has stolen it.'

The brothers protested. They were so sure that none of them had stolen anything that they said, 'If you find it in anyone's belongings then that person will be your master's slave.'

'Very well,' said the servants and they searched everybody's belongings and of course, they found the cup in Benjamin's sack.

The brothers were horrified. They had promised their father they would take care of Benjamin and bring him back but they had told the servants that the thief would be Joseph's slave.

There was nothing that they could do. They returned to Egypt and came before Joseph again.

Judah, one of the brothers spoke and pleaded with Joseph.

'Our father is old,' he said. 'He has many sons but two were especially beloved by him. One of these two was lost many years ago and now there is only Benjamin left. Please do not keep him to be your servant for it would surely kill our father. Keep me instead.'

## Joseph explains who he is

But Joseph could not contain himself any longer and he cried out, 'Look my brothers. It is me – Joseph. I am not dead but am alive.'

And he told them the story of what had happened to him. At first the brothers could not speak; they were overwhelmed with different feelings – joy and gratitude and also guilt and shame at what they had done.

But Joseph said to them, 'Do not worry any more for I forgive you all. Go and bring my father. Tell him I am alive and he can come and live in peace and contentment with plenty for him and for you all.'

And so the brothers did as they were asked and went to fetch Jacob. Jacob was overjoyed that Joseph was still alive.

'I will go and see him before I die,' he said.

And God spoke to Jacob and said to him,

'I am the God of your fathers. Go to Egypt and do not be afraid for I will make a great nation of you. I will be with you and I will bring you back again.'

And Jacob knew that everything was finally all right so he rejoiced and went to Egypt where he saw Joseph and finally embraced the son he thought he had lost.

# The story of Moses

Some years after the death of Joseph, a new king came to rule over Egypt. He did not know of Joseph and he felt threatened by the people of Israel who lived in Egypt. He was worried that they would want more power as there were so many of them and so he made them serve the Egyptians. As well as this, he decided that he would not allow any baby boys to live in case they threatened his power.

One day a baby boy was born to an Israelite woman. He was a beautiful baby and she loved him and so she hid him from the soldiers of Egypt.

She kept him safe for three months but as he grew bigger it was harder to hide him and so she made a little boat from rushes and laid the baby in it. Then she put the little boat in the reeds by the river.

A little later, the daughter of Pharaoh came down to the river to bathe. As she was walking by the riverside she saw the little basket boat and she told one of her maidservants to bring it to her.

When she saw the baby she was sorry for him and she said, 'I think this is one of the Hebrew women's babies.'

Her maidservant said, 'Shall I go and get one of the Hebrew women to be his nurse?'

And the Pharaoh's daughter agreed, so the maidservant went and fetched the baby's mother and said to her, 'If you take this baby and nurse it for me I will pay you.'

The mother was overjoyed that her son was to live and she agreed immediately. She did as she was asked and brought him back to Pharaoh's daughter when he was older and she adopted him as her own son.

'I shall call him Moses,' she said, 'because I took him from the water.'

## God speaks to Moses

When Moses was grown up, he could see that his own people were only servants in the land of Egypt and were not treated well. One day he saw an Egyptian beating one of his people and he was so angry that he killed the Egyptian. The Pharaoh was furious and wanted to kill Moses but Moses ran far away until he was safe.

Knowing that he was now safe, he married and settled down to help his father-in-law to care for their sheep. One day, while he was looking after the sheep, a very strange thing happened to him.

He was walking along with the sheep when he noticed a bush that was on fire, but although the bush was burning, it was not being burnt up. Moses was astonished and was going to have a closer look when he heard a voice. 'Moses,' it said. 'Take off your shoes for the place where you are standing is holy ground.'

Moses stopped, trembling. Whose was this voice? The voice spoke again.

'I am the God of your Fathers. I have seen that my people are suffering and I will free them. I want you to go to Pharaoh and tell him to let my people go free.'

Moses, hearing the voice of God coming from the middle of the burning bush, said to him. 'Who am I to go to the Pharaoh and say this? I am just an ordinary person.'

God answered him, 'I will be with you and when you have completed this task, you will serve me on this mountain.'

Moses replied, 'So I am to go to the sons of Israel and say to them, "The God of your fathers has sent me to you." What if they ask me what your name is? What shall I say?'

And God replied, 'You must say that I said I AM WHO I AM. Tell them that I am the God of Abraham and Isaac and Jacob.'

Moses wanted to believe but he was frightened that nobody would believe him and he would fail, so he said again, 'But what shall I do if they don't believe me?'

And this time God replied, 'Throw the rod you have in your hand on to the ground,'

Moses did as he was asked and the rod turned into a snake. He started to run away from it but God said, 'Now take hold of its tail.'

Moses grasped its tail and immediately it turned back into a rod. Then God told him to put his hand inside his coat and when he took it out again it was ugly and diseased. Then he put it back into his coat and when he took it out this time it was healthy and normal again.

'Tell the people about these two signs,' said God.

And finally Moses agreed to do what was asked of him.

Moses and his brother Aaron went to Egypt and asked the Pharaoh to let the people of Israel go free.

'The Lord our God has asked this,' they said.

But the Pharaoh would not listen. 'Who is this God of yours?' he said. 'I do not know him and will not let your people go free.'

Then he told his soldiers to make the Israelites work harder than before.

Moses spoke to God. 'Look what has happened,' he said. 'Our people are being made to work harder. Their life is worse since I spoke to the Pharaoh.'

And God promised Moses that he would change the Pharaoh's mind.

## The ten plagues

'I will send ten plagues on the Egyptians,' God said, 'and then the Pharaoh will change his mind.'

Then he told Moses to go to the river and to take the rod that he had turned into a snake. If the Pharaoh still refuses then you must stretch your hand out over the river. Moses did everything as God had said and still the Pharaoh refused to listen, so Moses stretched out his hand and the river turned into blood.

The Egyptian people were horrified but still the Pharaoh did not change his mind, so, seven days later a plague of frogs descended on Egypt. They went everywhere – into the houses and into all of the rooms where the Egyptians lived.

This was followed by a plague of lice and the wise men in Egypt spoke to Pharaoh and said, 'You must change your mind. This is God's work.' But Pharaoh was stubborn and refused to listen to anybody.

So God said to Moses, 'Go back to Pharaoh and tell him again that he must let my people go so that they can serve me or I will send swarms of flies into your land.'

Moses did what he was told but still the Pharaoh ignored the warnings and so the flies descended upon Egypt. Finally Pharaoh sent for Moses and Aaron and told them to go and make a sacrifice to God and plead with him to remove the flies. Moses and Aaron went into the wilderness and sacrificed to God and God listened and the flies vanished. They went back to Pharaoh expecting him to free the people but Pharaoh, once the flies had gone, did not want to free them.

So now God sent other plagues. The next one was to make all of the cattle and animals belonging to the Egyptians ill. Then he sent a plague where all of the Egyptians were covered with painful sores and next a plague of hailstones so big and powerful that many things were destroyed. The wise men tried to tell Pharaoh that he must let the people of Israel go free but still he refused.

Then a plague of locusts came down upon Egypt and they ate up many of the trees and plants on the earth and once again Pharaoh asked Moses and Aaron to go and plead with God for him and his people. God listened to Moses and the locusts left the land of Egypt but once again Pharaoh, when he had got what he wanted, refused to let God's people go free.

And so God sent two more terrible plagues. The first was a plague of darkness where, for three days, none of the Egyptians could see because it was so dark. And when this plague did not work God sent the last and most terrible plague.

## The Passover

God spoke to Moses. 'I want you to make this month the first month of your year. On the tenth day tell everybody to take a lamb. If a family is too small to use a whole lamb then they should join up and share with their neighbours. Keep it until the fourteenth day and then kill it at twilight. Take the blood and paint some of it on the two doorposts and on the lintel of the house. Then roast the lamb and eat it. You have little time so you must eat it with bread that has not risen and has no yeast in it and with bitter herbs. Wear your sandals and your belt and have your stick in your hand. This is my Passover because my angel will travel through the land and will strike down all the oldest children of the Egyptians. He will pass over your houses and he will know they are yours because you have the blood of the lamb on your doorposts. You must keep this as a feast for ever.'

And everything happened just as God had said. In the morning there was great sadness in Egypt and Pharaoh sent for Moses and said to him, 'Go, leave my land and take everybody and everything with you.'

So finally the people of Israel were free to leave Egypt with all their belongings and they followed Moses into the wilderness and God went in front of them as a pillar of cloud during the day and as a pillar of fire at night to lead them safely.

But, back in Egypt, Pharaoh began to regret his decision. 'I should never have let them go,' he said. 'They were good workers. Who will do their jobs now? We will have to pay people.'

So he decided to go after them. He collected his army and began to follow them. They had many horses and the Israelites were on foot so they caught up with them just as the Israelites reached the sea.

The people of Israel could see the army chasing them and they were afraid.

'We can't go any further,' they said. 'We have no boats and we can't swim across the sea. We'll all be taken back as slaves.'

But God had a plan. He was not going to abandon his people. He told Moses to stretch out his hand over the sea. Moses did this and, to everybody's astonishment, the waves rolled back and a dry path appeared in front of them for them to escape. The Israelites hurried along the path but the Egyptians followed them. They were catching them up.

As soon as the Israelites reached the other shore God told Moses to stretch out his hand again and, as soon as he did this, the sea flowed back over the path and the army of Pharaoh was swallowed up by the water. The Israelites were free.

## The people of Israel complain

Moses led the people through the wilderness for three days but soon they began to complain.

'We are thirsty,' they said, 'and there is no water to drink. All of the water here is bitter. What shall we do? We will die if we do not get any water.'

So Moses turned to God and God said to him, 'You see that tree, take it and throw it into the waters.'

Moses did as God asked and the water turned sweet so that the people could drink it. For a while they stopped complaining and followed Moses but soon they began to complain again because this time they were hungry and could find no food.

'At least we had food in Egypt,' they grumbled. 'We might have been slaves but we didn't starve.'

So Moses turned to God again and again God gave the people what they needed. He told Moses to wait until morning and when morning came, there was a heavy dew on the ground. When the dew lifted, the ground was covered with small round objects.

'What are those?' asked the people.

'That is the bread that the Lord has sent you,' replied Moses. 'Now, go and gather what you need and stop complaining.'

The people were satisfied and called the bread *manna*.

## Moses receives the Ten Commandments

Months after they had left Egypt the people of Israel came to Mount Sinai. Moses left the people and went up the mountain where God spoke to him.

'You will be a holy people,' said God. 'You are my treasure.' And God told Moses how he wanted them to live.

'I am your God,' he said. 'I want you to honour me and not to have any other gods. I do not want you to take my name in vain and I want you to keep the Sabbath, which is my special day, as a holy day.

You must respect your mother and your father and you must not take anyone else's life. You should not steal or take another person's husband or wife and you must not lie about your neighbours. You must not be jealous of what your neighbour owns and want his things for yourself.'

God went on to tell Moses about different things they should do to honour him, so that there would be justice and peace among his people. When he had finished speaking, Moses came down the mountain with all of these commands written on two tablets of stone.

Now he had been gone a long time and the people of Israel had begun to think that something had happened to him or he had left them alone in the wilderness. They did not know what to do so they had taken their gold jewellery, melted it down and made a golden calf. Forgetting everything that God had done for them, they danced around this calf and worshipped it, singing songs of praise to it. Moses heard the singing as he came down the mountain and he was so angry when he saw what was happening that he threw the tablets on the ground and they broke.

'How can you betray what you know to be true?' he demanded. 'You have ignored everything that God has done for you and lost faith so quickly. I cannot believe that you didn't have the strength and the patience to wait for me and to trust that everything would be all right.'

And the people were sorry for what they had done. They melted the calf and Moses went back to God and asked God to forgive them. God gave him the tablets again with his commandments written upon them.

After this, Moses led the people for many years. Finally, after all of their wanderings in the desert, the people arrived in Canaan, just as God had promised Abraham.

# The story of Joshua

## God helps Joshua and his people to cross the river

When Moses had died, God spoke to Joshua who was the son of a man called Nun who had helped Moses.

'I want you to lead my people now,' God said. 'I will make the same promise to you that I made to Moses but you must be strong and brave if you are to be the leader of my people.'

Joshua was proud to be chosen and began to lead the people on their journey. One morning they came near to the river Jordan and knew that they would have to cross it if they wanted to continue on their travels. The river was flowing fast and they knew that the water would be dangerous to cross because they had all of their children and belongings to get across. But they also had a very special thing with them. When God had given Moses the Ten Commandments on the stone tablets, he had told Moses to build a special container to hold them. They had called this special container the Ark of the Covenant. The covenant was another name for God's promise. God had promised the people that he would look after them and the tablets showed the way that God wanted his people to live. Now they carried this special container with them on their journey and it was very important to them. They did not want to lose it in the river.

When they were near the river, God spoke to Joshua again. 'Tell the priests who are carrying the Ark to go in front. When they reach the edge of the river they must walk into the river and stand just in the water. Then, I will make the river safe for you to cross.'

Joshua called for the priests to come and see him. When they arrived he told them what God had said. 'You must stand in the water and you must be at the front of all of the people.'

When they got to the water's edge, the priests went to the front of the crowd, carrying the Ark. Then, very carefully they stepped into the river. Immediately the water stopped flowing and the priests and all of God's people could cross the river with dry feet.

# The story of Samuel

Many years after the death of Moses there lived a young girl named Hannah. Hannah prayed to the Lord that she might have a son and the Lord listened to her prayer. When her son was born she named him Samuel and she took him to the priest who was called Eli, and asked him if Samuel could serve God. Eli accepted him and he served God with Eli.

One night, when Samuel was a boy, he was sleeping when a voice woke him. The voice was calling his name. He thought it was Eli, who was growing old and so he jumped out of bed and ran into his master.

'Here I am,' he said. 'You called me.'

But Eli shook his head. 'I did not call you,' he said. 'Go back and lie down.'

So Samuel went back to his bed and lay down but soon the voice called him again. He jumped up and ran into Eli.

'Here I am,' he said. 'What did you want? You called me.'

But again Eli said that he had not called Samuel and sent him back to bed.

Samuel went slowly back to bed, a little puzzled. He was sure that he had heard a voice calling his name. He climbed slowly back into bed and lay down and tried to go back to sleep. But then he heard the voice a third time.

'I know I heard it this time,' he muttered to himself. 'It must be Eli.' He went into Eli's room and said, 'I am here. You called me, I know, because I heard you.'

And suddenly Eli realised that it was God calling Samuel. He said to him, 'Go back and lie down and if you hear the voice again then say, "Speak to me, Lord, because I am your servant and I am listening."'

So Samuel went back to bed and this time when he heard the voice he replied as Eli had told him.

Samuel grew up knowing that the Lord was with him and throughout his life he helped his people to know God.

# The story of David

When Samuel was grown up, God wanted him to find a king for his people. He told Samuel to go a man called Jesse because he had chosen one of Jesse's sons to be the king. Samuel did as God asked, and went to Bethlehem and prepared a sacrifice. Then he invited Jesse and his sons to come and he blessed them.

Seven of Jesse's sons were there and they all stood in front of Samuel but God told him that none of these was the right person. So he said to Jesse, 'Are these all of your sons?'

'No,' replied Jesse. 'The youngest is still out in the field because he is minding the sheep.'

'Send for him and tell him to come here,' said Samuel.

So the youngest of Jesse's sons came to Samuel. His name was David.

When Samuel saw David he knew that he was the one that God had chosen.

At that time, the people of Israel were fighting with an enemy called the Philistines. One morning a great warrior strode out from the camp of the Philistines and called to the Israelites. He was a huge man, covered in bronze armour.

'Choose somebody to come and fight me,' he challenged. 'If your warrior wins then we will stop fighting you and will serve you instead.'

The Israelites were afraid because the warrior looked unbeatable and nobody came forward to fight him. Every morning he stepped out from the Philistine camp and made the same challenge but still nobody accepted it and stepped forward to fight for the Israelites.

David was still a young boy but his brothers were grown men and some of them were fighting in the army against the Philistines. One morning Jesse sent David to his brothers with food and drink. When he arrived at the camp he heard the warrior, whose name was Goliath, challenging the people of Israel.

'Who is going to answer him?' David asked. 'We must fight for what is right.'

The king of the Israelites at that time was called Saul and when he heard what David had said, he sent for him. When David arrived at Saul's tent David offered to go and fight the warrior himself.

'But you are just a boy,' answered Saul.

'I protected my father's sheep from lions and bears,' said David, 'and God always kept me safe. He will keep me safe now.

Saul gave him some armour and a bronze helmet and David went out. David was not used to the armour and found it harder to walk, so he took it off. Then he took his stout stick and chose five smooth stones from the stream and put them in his bag. In his other hand he carried his sling.

Goliath, the warrior, could not believe his eyes when he saw a young boy walking out to meet him and he sneered at David, saying he was too young to fight him.

But David stood his ground and answered boldly, 'I come in the name of the Lord, the God of Israel. He will keep me safe.'

And quickly he fitted one of the smooth stones into his sling, swung it around his head and fired it at Goliath. The stone hit him on the forehead and Goliath fell to the ground. David had beaten him with a single shot.

When the Philistines saw that their champion was dead, they ran away. The people of Israel praised David for saving them from their enemies.

And so David grew up and the Lord was with him and when he was a man he was anointed the king of Judah.

# The story of Solomon

When David was an old man he declared that his son, Solomon, should be the king after him. He called his son, Solomon, to him and gave him instructions to live his life following the laws given to Moses by God. Soon after this, David died.

Solomon loved God and tried to follow his ways when he was ruling the kingdom he had been given. One day God asked him, 'What shall I give you, Solomon?'

Solomon answered, 'You were good to my father David and you have made me king after him. But I feel as though I am only a child and I do not know enough to govern the people. I ask you to give me an understanding heart so that I can choose between good and evil for my people.'

God was pleased that Solomon had asked for this. 'You could have asked for riches or for success,' he said to Solomon, 'but you haven't. Because you have made such a good choice you will be both wise and understanding and because you did not ask for anything for yourself, I will also give you riches and honour.'

And Solomon thanked God and grew in wisdom and understanding and he ruled his people wisely.

When he had been king for four years he decided to build a great temple to God. It took many years to build for it was built with great care and was beautiful both inside and out. When Solomon had finished having the temple built and it was ready to be used, he blessed the people and dedicated the temple to God.

# The story of Elijah

### God helps Elijah escape from his enemies

Some time after Solomon was king there lived a man named Elijah who was chosen by the Lord. One day his enemies were chasing him and Elijah escaped into the wilderness. When he got there he was exhausted and afraid so he sank down on to the ground and said to God, 'Oh Lord, let me die.'

And he lay down and slept under a broom tree, waiting to die. But an angel came and touched him and woke him up. The angel said to him, 'You must wake up and eat and drink.'

Elijah saw a cake and a jug of water near his head so he did as the angel asked but then he lay down again, ready to die.

The angel came back a second time and woke him. 'You must eat,' said the angel, 'because you have a long journey in front of you.'

Elijah got up, ate and drank and then began to walk. He journeyed for forty days and forty nights until he came to a mountain called Horeb, the mountain of God. There was a cave there so he hurried in and spent the night in the cave hidden from his enemies and waited for God to help him.

While he was in the cave he heard God's word.

'Go out of the cave and stand on the side of the mountain,' said God. 'I will come to you there.'

Elijah went out and a mighty wind blew, so strong that it made the trees fall and the rocks break but God was not in the wind. After the wind came an earthquake but God was not in the earthquake. Then there came a fire and Elijah looked for God, but God was not in the fire. Just then, there came the sound of a gentle breeze and Elijah found that God was in the gentle breeze. And God spoke to Elijah and told him what to do to escape and be safe.

# The story of Elisha

## God helps Elisha support a widow

After Elijah had died, another man, who was called Elisha, carried on his work, telling the people about God. He helped many people, calling on God's power to heal and to help. One of these people was a widow who came to Elisha, very upset.

'My husband is dead,' she said. 'We owe money and we cannot pay it now. The person we owe it to is coming to take my two sons away and make them slaves because we cannot pay. Please help me.'

Elisha said to her, 'What have you got in the house?'

'Just a jar of oil,' she answered.

Elisha thought for a minute and asked for God's help.

'This is what you must do,' said Elisha, after he had thought. 'Go and borrow lots of jugs and jars and anything that will hold oil. When you have done that, shut the door and start to pour the oil into these jugs and jars.'

The widow did not know why she had to do that because there was only enough oil to fill one jug but she trusted Elisha and did as he asked. When they had collected lots of jugs and jars and basins they went back into the house and shut the door. The widow lifted the jug that held the oil and started to pour it into the first jar. Soon it was full. She looked into the jug, thinking that it surely must be empty but it was not and so she started to pour the oil into the next jar.

When this one was full she looked into the jug again. There was still lots of oil left. Hardly daring to believe what was happening, she started to fill the next jar . . . and the next. She went on until all the jugs and jars and basins that she had borrowed were full to the brim.

Elisha said to her, 'Now, go and sell the oil and you can pay what you owe.'

The widow thanked Elisha and praise God and then hurried off to sell the oil.

# The story of Daniel

## God helps Daniel escape from the lions

At one time there was a country where the Jewish people were forbidden to pray to their God. In this country was a holy man called Daniel. Daniel did not want to stop praying to God. He knew it was the right thing to do.

Other people did not agree though and they seized Daniel and took him to the king.

'Why are you still praying to your God?' demanded the king, angrily. 'You know it is against the law! You must stop immediately.'

But Daniel still refused to stop and so the king stood up.

'Take him to the lion pit,' he ordered. 'He has broken our law and must die. Throw him into the pit with the lions and then leave him.'

The soldiers did as they were ordered and Daniel was dragged off to the pit which was full of lions. The soldiers threw him down into the bottom of the pit and then left him there to be eaten.

The next day the king and his soldiers came back to the pit to see what had happened. To their amazement there was Daniel sitting in the bottom of the pit, alive and unhurt. The lions had not touched him. God had kept him safe.

Immediately the king ordered that Daniel should be lifted out of the pit. The soldiers did this and they all praised God for saving his follower.

# The story of Jonah

## God helps Jonah see what is the right thing to do

There was a great city called Nineveh but at one time the people who lived there were not good at all. God wanted to do something about this and so he spoke to a man called Jonah.

'I want you to go and speak to the people of Nineveh,' he said. 'They need to change their ways and stop doing wicked things. You must tell them this for me.'

Now Jonah was afraid. He did not want to go to Nineveh. He was afraid that nobody would listen to him. However, he also did not want to tell God that he wouldn't do what he had been asked and so he decided to run away. He went down to the seashore as quickly as he could. A ship stood there. It was almost ready to set off and it was heading for a place called Tarshish.

'I'd like to travel on your ship,' he said to the sailors quickly. 'I can pay for a ticket.'

The sailors agreed to let him travel and he rushed on board and sat down, his heart beating like a hammer inside his chest.

'Is anything wrong?' asked the sailors.

'Oh no,' answered Jonah quickly, getting to his feet and pretending to be interested in the sailors untying the ship.

Soon the ship was in the middle of the sea but there was trouble ahead. A wind began to blow and the sea grew chopp)y. The wind blew faster and the sea grew rougher and rougher until great waves were throwing the ship from side to side. The sailors were frightened and they decided that they needed to make the ship lighter.

'Quick,' they said to each other. 'Let's throw all of our cargo overboard. It's better to lose that than to lose our lives and maybe if the ship is lighter we will stand a better chance.'

They threw everything they could overboard but still the storm continued and the waves became bigger and more and more frightening.

Down below Jonah felt worse and worse. He knew that this was his fault. He should never have run away. Finally he gathered all of his courage and fought his way to the deck.

'This is my fault,' he shouted over the noise and uproar of the wind and waves. 'You must throw me overboard and then you will be safe.'

But the sailors were appalled and shook their heads. 'We will row harder,' they shouted back.

They went to their oars and put all their strength into rowing but it was no good. The sea grew wilder and wilder and the ship was tossed from side to side.

Jonah was frightened but he was even more convinced that the storm was his fault. Again he fought against the wind to reach the front of the boat.

'You have to listen to me,' he shouted. 'This is my fault because I didn't listen to what God was asking me to do. He wanted me to help and to do a special job. I didn't want to do it and ran away. You must throw me overboard and then you will be safe.'

Finally the sailors saw that they had no choice and they took Jonah and threw him into the sea as he had said.

But God was still looking after Jonah and he sent along a great fish. The fish swam up to Jonah and swallowed him whole.

For three days Jonah sat in the belly of the fish and he prayed to God, telling him that he was sorry for running away and asking for his help. God heard his prayers and three days after the fish had swallowed Jonah it swam to the shore and shot Jonah out of its mouth and onto the beach. Jonah could not believe his good luck. He had survived. Now he knew what he had to do and he went to Nineveh, just as God had asked him. He told the people that they needed to change their ways and be better than they had been. The people listened to Jonah and were sorry for all of the things they had done that were wrong.

# The Psalms
## Poems and songs to God

There are many psalms in the Bible, written for different reasons. Some of the poets wanted to praise and thank God while others needed to ask for help. Here are extracts from some of them.

## Poems of praise and thanks

### Psalm 1

Happy are the people who place their trust in the Lord.
They are like trees that are planted beside flowing water,
that produce fruit at the right time
and whose leaves never fade.
Everything they do will grow.
Anyone who follows God will have the light of life.

### Psalm 3

You, Lord, are a shield about me,
I speak to you and you answer.
I lie down to rest and sleep.
I wake up and the Lord looks after me.
I will not be afraid
even when lots of people are against me.

### Psalm 8

My heart rejoices in you, my Lord,
how great is your name throughout all the earth.
I look up at the heavens shaped by your fingers,
at the moon and the stars.
What are humans that you should think of them?
What are ordinary people that you should care for them?
And yet you have made them little less than a god.
You have crowned them with glory and honour.
How great is your name, O Lord our God, through all the earth.

## Psalm 18

Praise God who saves me.
The ways of God are perfect, his word is precious.
He protects everybody who comes to him.
I will praise you and sing songs to you.
You have shown your love for your children.

When I was sad I called to the Lord and he heard me.
I love you, Lord, with all my strength.
You are my rock and you keep me safe.
When things frighten me or I feel in danger, you are there.
Praise God who saves me.

## Psalm 19

The heavens proclaim the glory of God,
space shows us the work of God's hands.
Day after day tells us God's story;
night after night shows us God's word.
No voice is heard and yet God is present in all of his immense creation.
The laws of God are fair:
God's rule is to be trusted. It gives new life to your soul.
God's commands are clear. They give light to your eyes.
God's law is what we seek. It is sweeter than honey.
The heavens proclaim the glory of God.
They show the work of God's hand.
Day after day they tell God's story;
night after night they give God's message.

## Psalm 23

The Lord is my shepherd, I will not need anything.
He guides me in green fields and gives me rest.
He guides me along the right paths.
He is true to what he promises.
I will not fear any evil even if I walk in the darkest places
because he is there to comfort me.

## Psalm 32

Anyone whose mistake is forgiven is happy.
I have admitted my mistakes and you, O Lord, have forgiven me.
Let every good person pray to you when they are in need.
The flood waters may rise but they will not reach them.
You are my hiding place, O God.
You save me from being upset.
Anyone whose mistake is forgiven is happy.

## Psalm 33

The Lord fills the earth with his love.
Sing out your joy to the Lord;
praise him with your music.
The word of the Lord is faithful
and all his work is to be trusted.
God's plans will stand for ever.
The people who God has chosen for his own are happy.
The Lord loves justice and right
and he fills the earth with his love.

## Psalm 46

The Lord is with us, God gives us strength.
God is for us, somebody who protects us and makes us strong.
So we shall not be afraid even if the earth should rock
and the mountains fall into the depths of the sea.
God is within and cannot be shaken.
God will always help.

## Psalm 47

God is king of all the earth.
Everybody clap your hands and call out to God with shouts of joy
because the Lord is king of all the earth.
Our birthright is from God, God gives us our glory.
Sing praises to God forever.

## Psalm 65

We praise you, O God.
You care for the earth and give it water; you fill it with riches;
you provide seeds for the earth;
you level it and soften it with showers.
You crown the earth with goodness, it gives us plenty.

## Psalm 84

How lovely is your dwelling place, Lord, God of hosts.
My soul is longing for the house of the Lord.
My heart and soul ring out their joy.
The people who dwell in your house are happy.
They are forever singing your praise.
For the Lord our God is a shield.
He will give us his favour and glory.

## Psalm 90

Lord, you have always looked after us.
Before the mountains were born or the earth or the world created
you were there, without a beginning and without any end.
In the morning, fill us with your love and we will rejoice all day.
Let your glory shine on your children.
Let God's favour be with us
and give success to the work that we do.

## Psalm 96

Sing a new song to the Lord.
All the earth, sing to the Lord.
Sing to the Lord and bless his name.
Tell all the people about the wonders of the Lord;
tell all of the people about his glory.
The Lord is great and deserves our praise.
Let the heavens rejoice and all the earth be glad,
let the sea and everything within it ring out their praise.
Let the land and all it grows rejoice.
Let all the trees of the wood shout for joy.
God will rule the earth with justice
and will judge the people with truth.
Tell the nations that God is king.
He will judge the people fairly.

## Psalm 100

All the earth, cry out with joy to the Lord.
Serve the Lord with gladness;
come before God singing for joy.
Know that the Lord is God.
God made us and we belong to God.
We are God's people, the sheep of his flock.
How good God is;
God's love is forever.

## Psalm 104

My soul blesses the Lord.
Lord God, how great you are.
Dressed in majesty and glory and wrapped in light,
everybody looks to you to give them their food in season.
You give it, they gather it up, you open your hand and they have their fill.
You send forth your spirit and they are created
and you renew the face of the earth.

## Psalm 139

O Lord, you know me so well.
You are with me when I am awake and when I am asleep.
Wherever I go you are there.
If I climb the heavens you are there.
If I go to the sea's furthest end, you are there,
when I die you are there.
If I go to the ends of the earth you are there;
even there you lead me and guide me.
I thank you for the wonder of myself
and all the wonders of your creation.

## Psalm 146

I will praise the Lord all my days,
make music to God while I live.
It is the Lord who is faithful for ever;
the Lord who gives bread to the hungry.
The people who are helped by God are happy,
their hope is in the Lord.
The Lord made heaven and earth,
the seas and everything in them.
It is the Lord who is faithful forever;
who brings justice to people who are treated unfairly.
O my soul, give praise to the Lord.

## Psalm 150

Praise God in his holy place;
praise him in the mighty heavens;
praise him for his powerful deeds;
praise him for his outstanding greatness;
holy is the Lord God almighty.

Praise him with the sound of the trumpet;
praise him with your dancing;
let everything that lives and that breathes
give praise to the Lord.
Holy is the Lord God almighty.

# Poems asking for God's help and protection

## Psalm 17

Lord, listen when I speak to you,
I will try to tell the truth.
I am here, I call,
listen to my voice.
Guard me as the apple of your eye.
Hide me in the shadow of your wings.
Listen to my prayer when I ask for help.
I will not speak untruths.
I am here and I call; you will hear me, O God.

Turn your eyes to me and hear my words.
I shall be filled with the sight of your glory, O Lord.
Listen to me, O Lord, and hear my voice.
Lord, listen to my voice and hear my prayer.
I will not be untrustworthy.
I am here and I call: You will answer me, O God.
Show me your great love.

## Psalm 25

Lord, help me to know your ways.
Tell me what you want me to do, teach me how to live.
Help me to know what is true for you are my God.
Remember your kindness and the love you have always shown us;
remember me, because you are so good.
You show the path to people who go astray.
You guide us and teach us your ways.
To you, O Lord, I lift up my soul.

# Poems helping people to know what to do

## Psalm 37

Give the Lord a special place in your life.
Trust in God and God will act so that your justice will shine like a light.
People who tell the truth are wise
and their lips speak what is right.
God helps people in times of trouble.
They trust God and do what is right.
Turn away from evil and do good
for the Lord loves justice and will never desert his friends.

## Psalm 40

Here I am, Lord, I come to do what you want.
You do not want me to give you things
but to listen to you.
You do not want me to give you sacrifices
but to be here and do what you want.
I have not kept your fairness to myself
but have told people about your faithful help.
I have not hidden your love and truth from people.

## Psalm 85

I will hear what the Lord God has to say for his voice speaks of peace.
God's voice speaks of peace, peace for his people.
God's help is close for those who love him
and his glory shall be all around.
Mercy and faithfulness have come together
and justice and peace go hand in hand.
God will help our lives to be rich and the earth to give lots of fruit.
Where God is, there will be justice; and peace will follow where God leads.

## Psalm 112

Happy are the people who love the Lord.
They take delight in God's commands.
They are a light in the darkness for good people.
They are generous and merciful and fair.
They trust the Lord with a firm heart,
with a certain heart they are not afraid.
They give to the poor with an open hand,
their justice will be firm forever.

# The prophets of God
## God's holy people explain his message

The prophets were people who tried to help God's people understand what God wanted. They explained what God was saying to them at that time. They lived among the people and helped them in different ways, sometimes by doing things but also by explaining God's words and actions.

The words that follow are just a few of the wise things that these people said and did.

# The prophet Isaiah

*One of the great prophets was named Isaiah. He tried to help people know what was right and to see that God cared for them. Here are some of the things that he said.*

## Isaiah tells people what to do

Stop doing things that are wrong and learn to do things that are good. Search for justice and help people who are treated unfairly. Be fair to people who do not have much and who have no one to look out for them.

The time will come when many people will go up to the mountain of the Lord, to the house of the God of Jacob. He will teach us his ways and we will do what he wants. God will guide many people and they will turn away from violence and turn to peace. They will not need their sword or their spears any longer and they will turn them into ploughshares and into pruning hooks, things they can use to work the land. Countries will not fight against each other and there will be no more war.

This is what you must do – you must share your bread with the hungry, and look after the people who are poor and have nothing. Then, your light will shine out just as the sun in the morning. God will guide you all the time and you will be like a spring of water that goes on forever.

## Isaiah prophecies about things to come

And God himself will give you a sign. A young girl will have a child – a son. She will call him Emmanuel.

The people who walked in darkness have seen a great light. The people who walked in the shadow of death have had a great light shine upon them.

You, O God, have made people happy and have given us great joy because a child is born to us; a son is given to us and he will be called Mighty God, Prince of Peace.

## Isaiah talks to the people about peace

The wolf will live with the lamb and the calf and the lion cub will feed together. The cow and the bear will make friends and the little child will put his hand near a snake but he will not be harmed because the whole country is filled with news about the Saviour.

## Isaiah tells people of God's love

Listen to what God is telling us. 'I, the Lord your God, am holding you by the hand. Do not be afraid because I will help you. I will make rivers spring up on lands that have no water and I will put fountains in the middle of valleys. I will plant special trees in the desert.'

Listen to how much God loves us. This is what God is saying to us. 'Would a mother ever forget to love and care for her baby or one of her children? No, she would not and so I, your God will never forget you, my own chosen people.'

Listen to how great God's love is for us. 'The mountains may depart and the hills be shaken but my love for you will never leave you and my promise of peace with you will never be shaken.'

God's spirit is upon me because he has sent me to tell the poor that good things are coming. He has sent me to heal people who are sad and unhappy and to tell people who are in prison that they will be free.

The Lord says, 'Now I create a new heaven and a new earth and the past will not be remembered. Be glad and rejoice forever in the things I am creating because I create joy and gladness for my people.'

# The prophet Jeremiah

*Another of the prophets was named Jeremiah. He often warned the people about the things they had done wrong. These are some of the things he said about how they should act and about God's love for them.*

## Jeremiah tells people how they should behave

Hear the word of the Lord, everybody in Judah who comes to worship God. This is what he says. 'Stop doing things that are wrong and do the right thing. You must make the right choices and not be unjust towards strangers and people who do not have parents. You must not hurt others or follow strange gods and then you will be safe and will have a home with me.'

'Wise people should not show off that they are clever. Strong people should not boast about being strong and rich people should not think that this makes them important. No, if people want to boast then they should boast that they know me because I am the Lord and I will judge wisely and kindly throughout all the earth. The people who do this are my delight.'

## Jeremiah tells the people of the love of God and his promise to care for them

God has spoken to me and said this. 'I have loved you with an everlasting love. I will gather you with loving kindness and you will be happy. I will gather everybody, people who are blind or lame, men, women and children. I will turn their sadness into joy. I will make a new promise, a new covenant with my people. I will write my law on their hearts. I will forgive and forget their faults. They will be my people and I will be their God.'

# The prophet Ezekiel

*Ezekiel was another prophet. While he told the people how to behave and warned them when they were not living in God's way, he often told them about the love that God had for them and the promise he made.*

## Ezekiel tells the people to turn away from sin

You are responsible for what you do yourself. If somebody who has done many wrong things turns away from that way of life and is sorry, then he will live and his mistakes will be forgiven. So, turn away from the things that are wrong and get a new heart and a new spirit and choose the right path.

God said to Ezekiel. 'Go to the people and tell them that they are turning away from me and not following my ways. Tell them that I will rule over them. I will gather them from all the places where they are scattered and I will bring them into the wilderness. I will speak to them of my ways just as I did with their fathers in the desert. I will send away the people who choose the wrong thing and will gather the good people on my holy mountain. Then they will know that I am the Lord because I will bring them into the land of Israel just as I promised their fathers.'

## Ezekiel tells of God's promise to his people

God says, 'I will look for my flock just as a shepherd cares for his sheep. I will gather them together and bring them to their own land. I will feed them and heal what is broken. I will make them strong and they will be safe. I will chase away dangers and they will live in peace because I am the true shepherd. The trees will bear fruit and the earth will be rich. They will know that I, the Lord am with them and that they are my people.'

God says to his people, 'You have shown disrespect to me and so I will make my name holy among you so that everybody will know that I am the Lord. I will pour clean water over you and you will be cleansed. I will give you a new heart and put a new spirit in you. You will be my people and I will be your God.'

God said to Ezekiel, 'I will gather my people from the lands where they have gone and I will bring them together into their own land. Then they will be united and have one king. They will follow me alone because they will be my people and I will be their God. They will live in the land I promised to Jacob and they will settle there. I will make a covenant of peace with them and it will last forever.'

# The prophet Hosea

*A prophet named Hosea warned the people many times about straying away from God's path and not doing the right things. At the end of his book, he tells the people about God's great love for them and his wish for them to turn back to him.*

Hosea said to the people, 'Come, let us go back to the Lord. Ask God to take away the things you have done that are wrong and recognise that he is your God.'

Then God will say to you, 'Come back to me. Find the words to say you are sorry and come back to me for I love you with all my heart. I will help you to grow strong and healthy and you will have beauty and grace. I will care for you, my people, so that you will blossom.'

# The prophet Micah

*One of the things that the prophet Micah told people was how they should live. He talked about peace, just as Isaiah did. He prophesied that a great event would happen in Bethlehem in the future.*

## Micah tells the people about peace

Many people will come to God's house. Many countries will want to come to God and learn his ways and do what he asks. They will not need their sword or their spears any longer and they will turn them into ploughshares and into pruning hooks, things they can use to work the land. Countries will not fight against each other and there will be no more war. Instead, people will rest and will not be afraid. Other people follow their own gods but we will follow the Lord our God forever.

## Micah prophesies that Bethlehem will be great

And Bethlehem, even though it is small, will be very special because somebody will come from there who is to be the ruler of Israel. He will care for the people with God's strength and he will be great, right to the end of the earth. He shall be peace.

## Micah tells the people how to please God

God said, 'What have I done to you, my people? I have taken you from slavery and set you free. You give me sacrifice after sacrifice and yet this is what I want. I want you to be fair, to be forgiving and to be humble, walking in my ways.'

## Micah speaks of God's greatness

'Who else has a God like you? You forgive our mistakes and you are kind and generous to us. You take great joy in being kind. You keep your promises to our fathers.'

# The New Testament

The stories of Jesus and the Early Church

# The birth and boyhood of Jesus

The Jewish people had been waiting for a special person that God would send to help them. They called this person the Messiah and he would be the anointed one – God's special agent. This is the beginning of the story about how God sent his Son into the world to be the Messiah.

## The announcement of the birth of John the Baptist

When Herod was king in Judea, there was a priest named Zechariah who was married to a woman called Elizabeth. They were good people but sadly had not been able to have any children even though they both wanted a baby. One day, while Zechariah was in the temple performing his duties as a priest, an angel appeared to him. Now Zechariah was afraid but the angel spoke to him.

'Don't be frightened,' said the angel. 'God has heard your prayer and soon your wife Elizabeth will have a baby boy. You must call him John. He will be a very special person and will be filled with the Holy Spirit. He will help a lot of people make peace with God.'

But Zechariah could hardly believe what he was hearing.

'How can I believe this?' he said. 'My wife and I are both old people.'

The angel answered. 'My name is Gabriel, an angel of God, and I was sent to give you this good news. But because you will not believe me, you will not be able to speak until the day your baby is born.'

When Zechariah came out of the temple the people were amazed because he could not speak. He finished his service in the temple and then went home. Sure enough, his wife became pregnant and they waited for their baby to be born.

# Mary is visited by an angel

Now Elizabeth was related to a girl called Mary who lived in Nazareth. Mary was excited because she was engaged to a man called Joseph. Joseph was a carpenter and soon they were to be married. Now Mary was a very good person. She didn't boast or show off and she was kind and because of this God chose her to do something very special.

One morning she was at home when suddenly she saw a bright light and an angel appeared. She was frightened but the angel said, 'Don't be frightened. I've come to tell you that God thinks you are so special that he has chosen you to do a very important thing.'

Mary couldn't believe what she was seeing but the angel carried on,

'God wants you to be the mother of his son. You will have a baby and call him Jesus. He is a very special person who will grow up to do great things.'

Mary was amazed. She didn't think that she was so special. 'How can this be true?' she stammered.

'It is true,' answered the angel, whose name was Gabriel. 'You have been blessed by the Holy Spirit. And there is more because your relative, Elizabeth, who is an old lady, is also expecting a baby.'

'But she has wanted a baby for so long,' gasped Mary. 'She will be so happy.'

The angel smiled at her. 'God can make all things possible,' he said.

Mary bowed her head. 'I will do whatever God asks of me,' she said.

And when she looked again, the angel had gone.

# Mary visits Elizabeth

Mary rushed to visit Elizabeth and to share her good news. As soon as Elizabeth heard Mary's voice the baby inside her jumped and Elizabeth was filled with the Holy Spirit. She said in a loud voice, 'You are blessed among all women and your baby is blessed too. I can't believe that the mother of my Lord has come to visit me but as soon as I heard your voice, my baby leapt for joy.'

Mary answered her saying, 'My soul praises God who has done marvellous things for me.'

She stayed with Elizabeth for three months and then went home to Nazareth.

# John is born

When it was time for Elizabeth to have her baby she had a little boy. People could not decide what to call him so they were going to give him the same name as his father but Zechariah shook his head. He still could not speak but it was clear that he wanted to tell them something. Quickly someone brought him a tablet to write on and as soon as he received it, Zechariah wrote, 'His name is John.'

The minute he had written this he found that he could speak again and he praised God. Everybody was amazed and they looked at the baby boy and wondered among themselves, 'What kind of child is this? He must be very special.'

# Jesus is born

Meanwhile, in Nazareth, it was nearly time for Mary to have her baby but just as her time drew near, they got some news that was not very good. The Romans ruled over a lot of different places at this time and they wanted to know exactly how many people lived in the places they ruled. They told everybody to go back to the place that their family came from so that they could count them. This meant that Joseph had to travel all the way from his home in Nazareth to Bethlehem and because Mary was his wife, she had to go with him.

Now this was a very difficult journey for somebody who was having a baby but they set off and after a long time they arrived in the town of Bethlehem. More bad news was waiting for them here. Everywhere was full. Wherever they went trying to find somewhere to stay, the answer was the same. 'There's no room!'

Joseph was getting more and more worried. He could see that Mary was tired and that it would not be long before her baby would be born. Finally there was only one place left to try. Joseph knocked on the door but the answer was the same. 'Sorry, we're full.'

They were just turning away when the innkeeper called them back. He could see that Mary was close to tears and felt sorry for them.

'There's room in the stable if you want to stay there,' he said.

So Mary and Joseph stayed in the stable and that night, Mary's baby was born. She wrapped him in a blanket and laid him in the manger where the innkeeper kept the hay for the animals. They decided to call him Jesus.

Mary and Joseph were delighted with their new baby. Unknown to them, though, the news of their baby was spreading. In a field just outside the town, shepherds were looking after their sheep when they saw a bright light in the sky. Angels appeared and told them that a new baby had been born in the town of Bethlehem and that he was a very special baby.

When the angels had gone, the shepherds hurried to Bethlehem and found Mary and Joseph with baby Jesus. They congratulated them and gave them presents to celebrate his birth.

# The visit of the three wise men

While Mary and Joseph were taking care of their newborn baby, three very wise men were travelling from distant lands to find them. They were people who watched the stars and they had seen a special star which they knew meant that great things were about to happen. The appearance of this star told them that a new and very important baby was to be born and he was a great person.

As the star moved across the sky the three wise men followed it, travelling over hills and valleys until the star finally came to rest.

Because they were expecting a great king, the men first thought that it was telling them to go to the palace but when they got there they could see that no baby had been born. The king, who was called Herod, was suspicious and thought that the star meant that somebody was born who would grow up to overthrow him and take his kingdom away. He told the wise men to go and find the baby, then come back and tell him so that he too could go and honour him. Really he meant to go and kill the baby so that he would not be a threat.

The wise men went out and continued their search until they found the stable where Mary and Joseph were staying. They went in and gave gifts to the baby.

Just as they were about to leave to go back to their own countries, though, an angel warned them in a dream not to go back to the king. The angel told them that the king was waiting for them to return but they needed to go home a different way and not tell him about the baby.

The angel also warned Joseph and Mary that King Herod was planning to find their baby and kill him so they took him and escaped into Egypt where they lived until Herod died. When they heard that Herod was no longer a threat, they returned to Nazareth which was their home and Jesus grew up there.

# Jesus grows up

When Jesus was growing up Joseph and Mary would take him every year to Jerusalem to celebrate the Passover. When Jesus was 12 they went as usual but when it was time to leave to go home, Jesus stayed behind. Mary and Joseph thought he was with their family and friends and so did not worry until night when they started to look for him and realised that he was not with them. Frantic with worry they hurried back to Jerusalem to see if they could find him. When they got there they looked everywhere. Three days after they had realised he was lost they found him in the Temple. He was sitting with the teachers, asking questions and listening. Mary and Joseph rushed up to him.

'What are you doing? We've been so worried. Where on earth have you been?'

But the teachers who were sitting with him told them how amazed they were at his understanding.

Jesus was sorry he had upset Mary and Joseph but he said seriously, 'You don't need to worry. Don't you know that I must be about my Father's business?'

They did not understand what he meant. He got up and went home with them where he grew up, under their guidance and care.

# John the Baptist prepares the way for Jesus, and Jesus prepares for his ministry

When Jesus was grown to be a man, he knew that the time had come for him to begin his ministry and to spread the good news. Elizabeth's son, John, had also grown up and he told the people that a great person was coming.

## John the Baptist

Now Elizabeth's baby, John, was also growing up and he knew that he had been sent by God to deliver a special message to people. When he was old enough he went into the wilderness of Judea. He dressed in camel's hair and ate wild honey and locusts. He began to urge people to change their ways.

'Share what you have,' he said. 'Be sorry for the things you have done wrong and don't take more than your fair share.'

Lots of people came to him and listened to what he had to say and he baptised them in the River Jordan.

Some of the people began to ask who he was. 'Are you the Messiah – the Christ? Are you God's special agent?' they asked.

But John replied by quoting from the prophet Isaiah.

'*I am the voice of one who cries in the wilderness,*
*Prepare the way of the Lord.*'

Some of the people asked, 'Why do you baptise people if you are not the Christ?'

John answered them like this. 'I baptise you with water. There is someone coming soon who will baptise you with fire and with the Holy Spirit. I am not fit to even untie his sandal.'

# Jesus is baptised

While John was talking to people, Jesus came up. He went into the water and was baptised by John. As he came out of the water the heavens opened and the Holy Spirit came down in the form of a dove. A voice spoke from heaven, saying, 'You are my beloved Son. I am very pleased with you.'

The people were astonished and John said, 'I did not know him but I was told by the one who sent me that one day, I would see the Spirit descending upon somebody. On that day I would know that he is the one who will baptise you with the Holy Spirit. I can tell you that today I have seen that.'

# Jesus prepares for his ministry

After he had been baptised Jesus was led into the wilderness by the Spirit to be tempted by the devil. While he was there he fasted for forty days and forty nights. By this time he was very hungry.

Because he was so hungry the devil thought he would be weak. He wanted Jesus to follow him and turn away from God. So he came to Jesus and said, 'I know you are hungry! If you are the Son of God then you can turn those stones into bread and eat them. Then you will not be hungry.'

But Jesus was strong. He would not do what he was being tempted to do. Instead he said, 'The Scripture says that we do not only need bread. We need all of the words that come from God.'

Then the tempter took him into the holy city and set him down on the highest point in the Temple. He said, 'Why don't you jump off? If you are the Son of God then it says in the Scripture that God will send his angels to protect you.'

But Jesus was not fooled. He answered, 'It also says in the Scripture that you should not tempt the Lord your God.'

The devil tried for the last time to tempt him. He took him up a very high mountain and he showed him all the kingdoms of the world. He said to Jesus, 'I will give you all of this if you will just worship me.'

But Jesus was not deceived. He said, 'Get away from me Satan. It is written in the Scripture that you should worship God only and you should only serve him.'

Defeated, the devil left him and Jesus was cared for by angels.

# The ministry of Jesus

When Jesus had prepared for his ministry he spent three years travelling around spreading his message of good news and peace and living what he preached. He performed many miracles and good deeds and brought a new message of love and forgiveness to the people. The following sections are different things that happened during those three years.

# The beginning of the ministry of Jesus

Throughout his ministry Jesus wanted to make a difference to people and so he started his ministry by calling people from different jobs and places to be his special followers. He then travelled with them, helping others and showing them how to live.

## Jesus calls his disciples

As Jesus was walking along the Sea of Galilee he saw some fishermen called Simon and Andrew. They were working on their nets but when they saw Jesus they stopped because they knew that he was a special man.

Jesus looked at them and he knew that they were special people too. He knew that they were good people and would be good friends.

'Come with me,' he said to them. 'Follow me and I will teach you to help other people.' At once they left their boats and their fishing nets and they followed Jesus.

Further on he saw two other brothers called James and John. They were mending their nets too. He said the same thing to these two and they decided to follow Jesus too, so they left their boat and went with him.

Many other people followed Jesus and one day he called all of his followers and went up a mountain to pray. When he had prayed he chose twelve of his followers to be his special helpers. Their names were Simon, whom he called Peter, James and John, Andrew and Bartholomew, Matthew and Thomas, another man called James, a man called Thaddeus and another man called Simon. He also chose a man called Judas Iscariot. These were the twelve he chose to be his apostles.

# Jesus performs his first miracle

Soon after Jesus had called his disciples, there was going to be a wedding in a place called Cana. People had been getting ready for this wedding for a long time and they got more and more excited as the big day drew near. When the day arrived, Jesus went to the wedding along with his mother and some of his friends. They were enjoying themselves when Mary, Jesus' mother, suddenly noticed that there was a problem. The wine was running out. Before long there was none left.

Now this was a serious problem because the celebration was still going on and people wanted to enjoy a glass of wine. Mary thought about this problem. She could see that it was going to be very embarrassing for the people who were organising the wedding and so she decided that they needed some help. Going over to Jesus she said to him,

'They seem to have run out of wine. Do you think you could do something to help them?'

Jesus didn't really want to help at first because he knew that soon he would want to start travelling and helping lots of people and he was still getting ready for that but, because his mother had asked him, he agreed.

She went over to the waiters and said, 'You'd better do whatever Jesus asks you.'

There were six huge water jars made out of stone standing at the side. They were used to hold water for getting washed. Jesus told the waiters to fill them up to the brim with water. They did this and then he said,

'Now take a little bit out and give it to the head waiter.'

They did not really understand why but they did what he asked. To their astonishment, when the head waiter drank the water they had brought, it had turned into delicious wine.

The head waiter couldn't believe how nice it tasted. He went over to the bridegroom and said, 'I can't believe you've left this wine till the end. You should have served it at the beginning when people would have really appreciated it.'

It was only later, when people began to talk, that they realised that a wonderful thing had happened.

# Jesus meets a Samaritan woman

Jesus and his disciples set off for Galilee. They went through a place called Samaria and here Jesus stopped for a rest by a well. His disciples went into the city to buy food. While he was resting a Samaritan woman came up to get water from the well. Jesus spoke to her.

'Would you give me a drink?' he asked.

The woman was astonished.

'I thought all Jewish people did not like Samaritans,' she said. 'I'm surprised that you will speak to me. Most Jews wouldn't have anything to do with me. They think Samaritans are not worth talking to.'

But Jesus sat and talked with her for a long time and told her many things about God that she did not know. She listened and was amazed at how wise he was. When his disciples came back, she went off to tell everybody about him.

# Jesus returns to Nazareth and is rejected

When Jesus arrived in Galilee one of the places he went to was Nazareth where he had grown up. He went into the synagogue and read this to the people.

'I have been given the Spirit of the Lord. He has called me to bring good news to poor people and to set prisoners free. He has sent me to help blind people to see and to help people who are suffering.'

He closed the book and said to them, 'This is being carried out today, right now, while you are listening to me.'

Now the people did not like what he was telling them because he seemed to be saying that God was for everybody and not just for them.

'This can't be true,' they said. 'Surely this is just Mary and Joseph's son.'

And jumping to their feet they rushed at him, meaning to throw him from the top of the hill but he slipped through the crowd and walked away.

# The miracles of Jesus

One of the key messages that Jesus brought was that you should not just talk about doing good but should actually do it. Changing the water into wine was the first miracle that Jesus performed but this was the first of many. He wanted to make a difference to the people he was teaching and so many of these miracles were to heal them from sickness and disease.

The following stories are about some of the people he helped.

# Jesus heals many people

## The nobleman's son

Jesus came to Cana in Galilee where he had turned the water into wine. There was a nobleman who lived there and his son was very sick. When the man heard that Jesus had arrived he hurried to find him and, when he did, he begged him to come and heal his son because he knew that soon he would die. Jesus stopped when the man came up and spoke to him. He could see that he was very upset. He spoke to the man and said, 'You can go home. Your son is well.'

The man rushed home but before he reached his house he saw one of his servants racing towards him.

'Your son is well,' he gasped as he reached him.

'What time did he get well?' asked the nobleman.

And when the servant told him, he knew that it was the exact time that Jesus had told him that his son was well. From that day he and his entire household believed in Jesus.

# The man who was possessed

Jesus went to another town in Galilee called Capernaum. He went into the town and taught the people there. The people who heard him were amazed at what he said.

'His words make so much sense,' they said to each other. 'He speaks so well.'

Now in this town, in the synagogue, there was a man who was seized with a madness. This sickness made him shout out, 'Leave us alone, Jesus of Nazareth. I know who you are. You are the Holy One of God. Have you come to destroy us?'

But Jesus told the madness to leave the man and it obeyed him. The man was cured. The people were even more astonished.

'How can this be?' they said. 'He has such power!'

# Simon Peter's mother-in-law

Jesus came out of the synagogue and went to Simon Peter's house. Now Simon's mother-in-law was suffering from a high fever and everybody was worried. When Jesus arrived they turned to him for help.

'Can you do something for her?' they asked. 'You can see how she is suffering.'

So Jesus went up to her and bent over her and told the fever to leave her. As soon as he did this the fever left her and she sat up, healed. She was so grateful that immediately she got up and began to serve him.

Many other people came to him to be healed that day and he laid his hands on them and cured them all.

# The man who suffered from leprosy

Jesus carried on travelling around, teaching the people and curing them from their illnesses. One day a leper came to him and begged him to cure him.

'I know you can do it,' he pleaded. 'I know you can make me well if you want to.'

Now Jesus knew that you catch leprosy by touching people who already have it but this did not stop him. He stretched out his hand saying, 'I do want to. Be healed.' And he touched the leper.

Immediately the man was healed. He was overjoyed but Jesus said to him, 'Go and show yourself to the priest but don't say anything to anyone else.'

The man left but he was so happy and excited that he could not stop himself from telling everybody about what Jesus had done for him.

# The man who was paralysed

Crowds of people often came to hear Jesus speak and one day there was such a crowd that nobody else could get into the house he was preaching in. Four men had brought one of their friends who was paralysed because they hoped that Jesus would cure him, but they could not even get in the door. So they had an idea and, climbing onto the roof of the house, they took some of it away and lowered the man on his stretcher through the gap. Jesus saw what was happening and he was impressed by the faith the friends were showing. He said to the man who was paralysed, 'Son, your sins are forgiven.'

Some of the scribes who were sitting nearby started to mutter to each other. 'Why does he say that? Only God can forgive sins.'

Jesus heard them and said to them, 'Is it easier to say that your sins are forgiven or to tell this man to get up and walk? Now, so that you understand that the Son of Man has the power to forgive sins, watch.'

And turning to the man who was paralysed he said, 'Get up, take your bed and walk back to your house.'

Immediately the man stood up and picked up his bed. He began to walk. The people were amazed at what had happened.

'We have never seen anything like this before,' they said.

# The lame man by the pool

Jesus went up to Jerusalem because there was a feast for the Jews. In Jerusalem there is a pool by the Sheep Gate and it is called Bethesda because it has five porches. Lots of very ill people lay there waiting for the waters to move because at certain times, an angel went down into the pool and stirred up the water. The first person to enter the water after this was healed and made well, so they were all hoping it would be them.

Now there was a man there who had been ill for thirty-eight years and Jesus saw him. He knew that the man had been suffering for a long time.

'Do you want to be made well?' Jesus asked him.

'Oh yes, sir, I do,' answered the man, 'but the problem is that there is nobody to help me into the pool. It takes me such a long time to get there that by the time I have reached the water somebody else has always managed to get there first.'

Jesus said to him, 'Get up then. Take your bed with you and walk.'

Immediately the man was made well. He got up and, carrying his bed, walked away.

This all happened on the day that they called the Sabbath. The Sabbath was the name for the holy day every week when people went to Church and rested so that they could praise God. It was against the law to do any work on this special day so when the Jews saw the man carrying his bed, they told him that he should not be doing it. But he told them what Jesus had done.

'Where is this man who healed you?' they asked.

But the man did not know who had healed him because Jesus had slipped away in the crowd.

Later Jesus saw the man in the Temple and spoke to him. The man recognised him and went to tell the Jews that this was the person who had healed him.

But many of the Jews were angry and began to plot against Jesus because he had broken their laws and worked on the Sabbath.

# The Jews challenge Jesus about the Sabbath

Now, one Sabbath day, Jesus took a walk through some cornfields. His disciples were hungry and picked some of the corn to eat. The Pharisees saw this and complained.

'That is forbidden on this holy Sabbath day,' they said angrily. They were hoping to catch Jesus out but Jesus did not get angry. Instead he answered them very wisely by quoting the Holy Scriptures.

Then he said, 'You should know that the Son of Man is master of the Sabbath.'

# Jesus heals on the Sabbath

After this, on another Sabbath day, Jesus went into the synagogue and began to teach. There was a man there who had a very poorly hand. Jesus knew that he could make this man's hand better but he also knew that some of the people were watching him to see whether he would do it and break the rule about working on the Sabbath or whether he would wait until the next day. The people waited and watched to see what he would do.

Jesus thought for a moment and then said to the people who were watching him, 'Doing something good on the Sabbath is not against the law. It is more important to help.' Then he asked the man to stretch out his hand and he healed him.

# The blind men

Jesus was walking along one day when he heard two men shouting to him. They caught up with him and he stopped. These men were blind.

'Be kind to us, Lord,' they said.

'Do you really think that I can help you?' Jesus asked.

'Oh yes, sir, we do,' they answered.

Jesus stretched out his hands and touched their eyes. As he did so he said, 'You deserve this because you have a lot of faith. You believe in me.'

As he touched their eyes and said this, they realised that their blindness had gone and they could see again.

They were overjoyed.

Jesus said to them, 'I don't want you to tell anyone else what I've done. Keep it to yourselves.'

But they were so excited that they couldn't help talking about it to everyone they met.

# The ten lepers

At this time there were a lot of serious diseases that nobody could cure. One of these was leprosy. Anybody who became infected with leprosy had to move away from other people because it was very easy to catch it. Other people stayed away from them because nobody wanted to be near them. They were afraid.

Now one day Jesus was on his way to Jerusalem when he saw not one leper but ten of them. Most people would have run away at once but Jesus didn't. Even though he knew he might catch the disease he didn't walk away. Instead he stopped and let them come up to him.

The lepers were amazed. They asked Jesus to help them. Jesus told them to go and show themselves to the priests. They did this and, as they did, they were cured. They were so delighted that they forgot the help they had been given and began to celebrate. One of them, though, did not forget. He came back to find Jesus and, when he did, he threw himself down and thanked Jesus, praising him for his goodness.

Jesus was glad that the man had come but he said, 'Did I not cure ten? Where are the others? Stand up and go on your way. Your faith has saved you.'

# The man who had been blind from birth

There was a man who had been blind ever since he was born and the disciples brought him to Jesus. Jesus made a paste and put it on the man's eyes and then told him to go and wash it off in a nearby pool. The man did this and as soon as he had washed away the paste, he realised that, for the first time in his life, he could see.

As he hurried away from the pool other people saw him and wondered.

'Isn't that the blind man?' one of them asked.

'No, it's just somebody who looks like him,' said another.

'It is me,' cried the man, filled with joy. 'I have been healed. I can see!'

The people were very excited. 'Where is this man who healed you?' they asked.

But the man who had been healed could not tell them.

# Jesus performs other miracles

## Jesus raises a widow's son from the dead

Jesus went to a town called Nain and when he got there he saw a funeral procession. A young man had died. Jesus saw that the young man's mother was walking by the side of her son's body and she was very upset. Her husband had also died and she was a widow. Jesus was sorry for her and the other people who were there so he went up to the young man and put his hand on the body. He said, 'Young man, I tell you to get up.'

To the amazement of the crowd, the young man sat up and began to talk to his mother. She was overjoyed and thanked Jesus.

The people were filled with wonder and said, 'God has visited his people.'

## Jesus makes the sea calm

One day Jesus got into a boat with his disciples and said, 'Let's cross over to the other side of the lake.'

So the disciples set sail and Jesus settled down in the boat. Soon he grew tired and fell asleep. While he was sleeping a great wind began to blow and a storm blew up. The boat was thrown from side to side and water began to seep in. The disciples were terrified. They thought that they were going to die.

They staggered over to where Jesus was still sleeping and shook him saying, 'Master, please wake up. The boat is going to sink.'

And Jesus woke up and looked at the bad weather. Then he spoke to the wind and the sea and told them to be still. Immediately the wind dropped and the sea became calm.

The disciples were astonished and whispered to each other, 'Who can he be? Even the wind and the sea do as says.'

# Jesus raises Jairus' daughter from the dead

A man called Jairus lived at this time and he had a daughter whom he loved very much. One day the little girl grew sick. He was very worried and sat by her bed, hoping she would get better but she got more and more ill. Eventually the little girl died and man was overcome with grief. 'What will I do now?' he said to himself. 'My little girl is gone.'

He had heard about Jesus and how he was travelling around helping people so, hardly daring to hope, he went to find him.

'I know he can help me,' he said again and again. 'I just need to find him.'

He hurried through the town looking for Jesus until he saw a crowd gathered and he hurried up to the people. Jesus was in the centre. Jairus rushed up to him.

'Please help me,' he gasped. 'My little girl has just died but if you come and lay your hand on her, I believe that she will live again.' Jesus went into the house.

'She is not dead; she is just asleep,' he said,

He took the little girl by the hand and she stood up.

Jairus was overjoyed and tears of joy rolled down his cheeks. 'I don't know how to thank you,' he stammered, hugging his daughter.

The people who had seen what had happened were astounded and news about Jesus spread.

# Jesus feeds five thousand people

A big crowd of people followed Jesus. They followed him a long way and sat and listened to him for a long time. Jesus taught them many things.

It got to be dinner time and everybody began to get hungry but they were a long way away from town and there was nowhere for anybody to buy any food. Jesus told his disciples to ask the people if anybody had anything to share. They asked a lot of people but only one little boy had anything. He had brought some bread and some fish.

Jesus asked the little boy if they could share it. The boy said that they could and gave the food to Jesus. Jesus took the food and blessed it. Then he told the disciples to share it out among the thousands of people. The disciples couldn't quite believe what he was asking them to do. They knew that the boy had only given Jesus a little food but they did as Jesus asked and began to share it out. To their astonishment there was plenty of food for everyone.

By the time they had finished everybody had enough and there was even some left over. The people were amazed and wanted to make Jesus a king but he slipped away into the mountains.

# Jesus walks on water

After Jesus had fed all of the people with the loaves and the fish, he went away by himself to be peaceful. The disciples went down to their boat and got in and rowed away from the shore. They had been rowing for a while when the wind began to blow and the sea grew very choppy. Just then they saw someone coming across the water towards them. They rubbed their eyes, thinking that the wind and the weather were playing tricks on them but soon they could see clearly that a man was walking across the water towards them. They were afraid but as he got closer they heard Jesus' voice say, 'Don't be frightened. It's me.'

Straight away they rushed to welcome him into the boat and soon arrived at the shore.

# Jesus raises Lazarus from the dead

In a town called Bethany there lived three friends of Jesus: Lazarus, Martha and Mary. One day Lazarus grew sick and Martha and Mary sent a message to Jesus, saying,

'Lord, Lazarus is ill.'

When Jesus heard this he finished what he was doing and, two days later, set off to go to Bethany.

By the time he arrived Lazarus was already dead. Martha rushed out to meet him. She was very upset.

'Lord, if you'd come straight away then this wouldn't have happened. Lazarus wouldn't have died.'

'Take me to him,' said Jesus.

Martha led the way to the tomb, calling for Mary, her sister, to come with them. Mary hurried out to join them along with the friends who had been taking care of the two sisters.

When they arrived at the tomb, Jesus told them to roll the stone away from the entrance. Wondering what he was going to do, the people did as he asked.

Then Jesus prayed to his Father and when he had finished his prayer, he called out in a loud, clear voice, 'Lazarus, come out.'

The people watched in astonishment and fear. What was going to happen? They heard a noise from inside the tomb and suddenly Lazarus came walking slowly out. He was still wearing the cloths they had wrapped him in when they had buried him.

'Help him take off the cloths,' said Jesus.

Martha and Mary were overjoyed and rushed to help him. The people who saw what happened were amazed. A lot of people believed in Jesus because of what they saw that day.

# Jesus is transfigured

When Jesus went to pray to his Father one day, a strange and wonderful thing happened.

Jesus went up a mountain and took with him just Peter, James and John. When they reached the top Jesus went to pray and the disciples settled down a little way off. Before long Peter noticed an amazing thing. He seized James and John and they watched in amazement and wonder. As Jesus had been praying his clothes had become dazzling white and his face shone like the sun. Then they saw two men who appeared and spoke with him. They knew it was Moses and Elijah.

After a while everything faded and when they looked, Jesus was alone and looked just like himself.

At first they did not know what to say. They wanted to build something to show where this wonderful thing had happened. But then, while they were standing there, a cloud came over their heads and they heard a voice. It said, 'This is my Son whom I love. Listen to him.'

They came down the mountain knowing that they had seen something very wonderful.

# Jesus brings a new message and teaches the people

Jesus wanted people to understand that God loved them and that they should love each other. He wanted them to learn a new way of living. He taught the people about this new way of living in many different ways – through direct teaching, through stories that had a special meaning and through his actions. He taught them in many different places and at many different times. Here is a collection of some of the things he said to them to help them to understand.

# Jesus teaches the people through words

## Jesus goes up a mountain to teach the people

Jesus saw that a great crowd had come together to listen to him and so he went up a mountain. The great crowd gathered around him and he sat on the grass with them all around, listening. He began to speak to them about happiness.

'You think that rich people are the happy ones,' he said, 'because they have everything they want, but you're wrong. It's people who want the right things who are blessed; they will get what they want.'

The people listened as Jesus went on, 'Anybody who forgives somebody else will be forgiven themselves when they say sorry. People who make peace will be called the children of God. All of these people will be happy.

And other people, the ones who are gentle and the ones who really mean what they say and do; the ones who are pure in their hearts; all of these people will be blessed.

When people call you names or are unkind to you because you follow me, you're blessed because you will get a great reward in heaven.'

The hillside was silent. Only the sound of Jesus' voice could be heard as the people sat, listening to everything he said. He went on, 'When you get upset or angry, don't make things worse by carrying on an argument. Try to make peace and give your friendship freely.'

Jesus stopped and thought for a moment and then went on, 'You should treat others just the way you would like them to treat you. What do I mean by this? Well don't judge them and then you won't be judged yourself. Don't criticise them and then you won't be criticised yourself. Forgive them and you will be forgiven. Give gifts to them and you will receive gifts.

Try to live like this. Be kind to each other just as your Father in heaven is kind to you. Don't complain about things that other people do wrong. First take a look at yourself and the things that you might do wrong. Take responsibility for your own actions before you try to help somebody else with their mistakes.'

The people sat and listened to all of these things that Jesus was saying. Some of them thought about how they had behaved in the past and felt ashamed. The things that this man from Galilee was saying made so much sense. It made them feel differently about themselves.

Jesus looked at the people and thought for a moment. He said, 'No one lights a lamp and then puts a bucket over it or hides it in a cupboard. No, you put a lamp on a lamp stand so that it lights up the whole room and people can see it when they come in. You are the light of the world. You must not hide and just look after yourself. You must let other people see how you shine. You are like salt – the salt of the earth. Without salt things are tasteless.'

Jesus looked at the people before going on, 'So you must be careful that you don't only pretend to be good on the surface. If you're going to church or doing something that's good and you remember that you have fallen out with somebody, then go back and make friends before you carry on.'

The people sat silently, drinking in the words of this man who sat before them. They wanted to hear more.

'I want to give you a new message today,' said Jesus. 'I know you have been told that if people hurt you or upset you, you should do the same thing back to them but I don't want you to do that. Instead, if somebody hurts you, don't hurt them back. If they ask you for something, then give them a bit more than they ask for. You see, you already know that you should love your friends but I'm telling you something new. I want you to try to love your enemies too. Try to care about everybody and not just the people who care about you and when you do things for other people, don't do them in front of everybody, just so that people will say how good you are. Do them quietly and don't make a fuss.'

Jesus smiled and went on, 'You see, it's not the people who say great things and talk a lot about being good that are doing the right thing. It's the people who actually do it.'

Jesus was giving the people a lot to think about. Some of the things he was saying were very new. They wondered if they should they believe him but as they listened they knew that they should. He spoke to them with so much knowledge and understanding

So Jesus went on, 'Anyone who listens to my words and follows them will be like a sensible man who builds his house on rock. When the rain and the floods come, the house will stand firm and will not fall down. Anyone who listens to my words but does not follow them is like a foolish man who builds his house on sand. When the rain and the floods come, this house will collapse.'

He looked at the people and then said. 'Let me tell you about praying to God your Father. When you want to pray, do it like this: Don't use words that mean nothing. Your Father in heaven knows what you want so when you pray, pray like this:

*Our Father in heaven, may people treat your name as a holy name. May what you want be done on earth just the way it is in heaven. Give us what we need today and forgive us for the things we have done wrong, just as we will forgive people who have done wrong things to us. And we ask you to keep us safe from harm.'*

# Jesus teaches people about what is important

A man came to Jesus and asked him this question. 'Lord, what do I have to do if I want to have eternal life?' Jesus said to him, 'You must follow the commandments. You must be truthful and honest, you must not hurt people with words or actions and you must love other people as much as you love yourself.'

## Who is the most important?

Jesus and his disciples made their way through Galilee, heading for Capernaum. On the way the disciples started to argue. They did not want Jesus to hear so they argued quietly but when they got to Capernaum Jesus said to them, 'What were you arguing about on the road?'

They did not want to tell him because they had been arguing about which one of them was the most important and they felt a bit ashamed. Jesus told them to sit down.

'You want to know who is special?' he said. 'Well listen to me. You know those people who don't boast and show off; the ones who don't push themselves forward all the time?'

The disciples nodded.

'Well, they are special,' he said. Then he took a little child who was nearby. He laid his hand on the child's shoulder and said, 'Anybody who welcomes a little child welcomes me.'

## The most important commandments

Another day a different person asked Jesus a question. 'Which are the most important commandments?' was the question.

Jesus answered, 'There are two important commandments and they are to love God with all your heart and to love other people as much as you love yourself. There is nothing more important than this.'

## Help one another

Jesus said to his friends, 'God will say to people, "You looked after me when I needed you to. You gave me food when I was hungry; you were kind to me when I had no friends; you looked after me when I didn't feel well."

'And then,' Jesus went on, 'people will ask God, "When did we do these things? We never saw you." And God will say, "Whenever you did these things for somebody else, you were doing them for me."'

# Jesus tells us that it is important that we listen to him

Jesus said to the people, 'John the Baptist came to you and he was like a lamp, shining brightly. Now I have come and what I am telling you is even more important because my father has sent me to do great things.'

## Martha and Mary

Jesus came to a village and went to the house of two sisters called Martha and Mary. He spent some time with them, talking to them. Now Martha was very busy while he was there, serving food and clearing away but Mary just sat and listened to Jesus. Martha got annoyed, asking Jesus to tell Mary to help her but Jesus said, 'Mary has made a good choice because she is listening to the things I have to say. She has seen what is important – to listen to my words.'

## I am the bread of life

The people asked Jesus, 'What do we have to do if we are to do the works that God wants?' Jesus answered them like this. 'This is what you must do, you must believe in the person that God has sent.'

The people then asked Jesus, 'What sign will you give us to show that you are the person that God has sent? Our fathers were given special bread when they were hungry in the desert.' Jesus said to them, 'I am the bread of life. If you come to me and believe in me you will never be hungry or thirsty.'

## My Father is always with me

Jesus said, 'I do not do anything by myself. I am telling you what my Father has told me. He sent me and he is always with me. He has not left me by myself because I always do what pleases him. If you try to listen to my words and live by them you really will be my disciples. You will learn the truth and the truth will make you free.'

## I am the light of the world

Some people, though, did not like what Jesus was saying and they criticised him. Jesus said to these people, 'People that belong to me listen to my voice. I know them and they follow me. I give them life and they will never be lost. No one will ever take them from me.'

Jesus said to his friends, 'Whoever believes in me also believes in God, the one who sent me. I am the light of the world. I have come into the world so that anyone who believes in me and follows me does not need to be in the dark any longer.'

# Jesus shows that everybody is special to God, no matter what they have done

Jesus talked to his friends. 'Do you know how very precious you are? In the market place you can buy five sparrows for a penny and yet not one is forgotten by God. If this is so, think how much more important you are. I tell you now, every hair on your head has been counted.'

He tried to explain to the people how important they were to God. 'What parent among you would give your children a stone if they asked for bread? None of you would, of course. You would be very sure of that. Well, you can be just as sure that your Father in heaven will give you his Holy Spirit if you ask him. If you ask then things will be given to you; if you search then you will find: if you knock, the door will be opened to you.'

# Jesus teaches the people through example

## Jesus forgives a woman who had sinned

Jesus went for a meal at somebody's house. When he sat down a woman came in. She had heard that Jesus was there and so she brought a jar of expensive cream with her. She knelt down at Jesus' feet. She was crying because she had made a lot of mistakes in her life and now she was sorry. Her tears fell on his feet and she wiped them away. Then she smoothed the cream over them.

People were shocked that Jesus would allow this woman near him for she had not been good, but Jesus said, 'Nobody else offered to wash my feet or greeted me with a kiss and yet this woman has done both.'

He turned to the woman and said gently, 'Your sins are forgiven. Go and be at peace. Live a good life.'

## Jesus chooses Zacchaeus

Jesus went into a place called Jericho and a lot of people came to hear him speak. A man called Zacchaeus was there but he was so small that he could not see Jesus, so he climbed a tree. Now Zacchaeus was a tax collector. He didn't have any friends. Nobody really liked him because he cheated them. When Jesus came to the tree he stopped and looked up.

Zacchaeus was worried. What would Jesus say? Would he tell him to go away because he was a cheat?

But Jesus surprised him. He looked at Zacchaeus and said, 'Come down, Zacchaeus. I would like to eat at your house today.'

Zacchaeus was overjoyed. He came down and hurried home to welcome him. He said to Jesus, 'I'm sorry that I've cheated people. I'm going to try to put things right.'

# The Parables
## Jesus teaches the people through stories

Lots of people followed Jesus and he tried to teach them different things to make their lives better and to make them think about the way they were living. He wanted to find a way to give his message that the people would understand and so he often told them stories that had a special meaning. These stories were called parables.

## The parable of the sower and the seed

Jesus told people this story.

'There was once a man who went out and sowed some seeds. While he was sowing, some of the seed fell on the edge of the path and the birds flew down and ate it.

He carried on sowing and some fell on rocky ground. There was not enough goodness there for the seed to grow and it did not grow strong enough, so it died.

He carried on sowing and now some seed fell into thorns and the thorns grew up around the seed and choked it.

He carried on sowing and some of the seed fell on rich soil. This seed took root and began to grow. It grew bigger and stronger and finally grew into fine, healthy plants.'

## The parable of the mustard seed

Jesus used to talk a lot about what it would be like if everybody lived in the right way. Sometimes, when he talked about this, he would tell them about the kingdom of God. One day he asked them, 'What do you think the kingdom of God is like?' The people didn't know so Jesus described it like this.

'I will tell you,' he said. 'It is like a mustard seed.'

Now of course Jesus didn't mean that it looked like a mustard seed because a mustard seed is tiny, so he explained it a bit more.

'When you plant a mustard seed,' he said, 'it is tiny. But – when it starts to grow it gets bigger and bigger until it becomes a big shrub and puts out big branches. That is what the kingdom of God is like.'

# The parable of the workers

Another time Jesus explained the kingdom in this way.

'The kingdom of God is like a farmer who went to hire some people to work on his farm. He agreed to give them a valuable coin for their wages. They worked all day. Later on, when they had been working for half a day, the farmer sent some other people to work with them. At the end of the day the farmer paid them and he gave them all the same wage. They all got one valuable coin. The people who had worked the longest grumbled that they should have got more but the farmer said, "Why are you grumbling? I gave you what we agreed. Don't be jealous. It's not your business what I do for these other people."'

# The parable of the good Samaritan

One day when Jesus was teaching, a man stood up who was an expert in the law.

'What do I have to do to gain eternal life?' he asked

Jesus answered him by asking him a question. 'What is written in the law?' he said.

The man replied, 'You must love God with all your heart and soul and you must love your neighbour as yourself.'

'That is right,' Jesus answered. 'If you do that you will have eternal life.'

But the man wanted to question Jesus even more.

'But who is my neighbour?' he asked.

In reply, Jesus told this story.

'A man was travelling one day when he was attacked by thieves. They stole everything he had and beat him. They left him lying on the side of the road, too injured to get up and help himself. All he could do was lie there and hope that somebody kind would come and help him.

Before long he saw somebody coming. As he got closer he recognised him. He knew that he was a very important person; somebody who spent a lot of time telling other people how to behave and what was right and what was wrong. As soon as this important person saw the injured man lying in the street, though, he pretended that he hadn't noticed him and he crossed the road and carried on walking.

The man lay there a little longer. He was getting weaker, when somebody else came along. His hopes rose because this too was an important person. This person's job was to teach people about important things and the way to treat others.

The injured man could not believe it when this man too crossed the road and pretended not to notice him.

The man was very weak now and had almost given up hope when he saw another person coming. As he got closer he realised that this man came from a different area called Samaria. Nobody liked the people who came from this area because they were different.

The man lay down and closed his eyes. It was no good. He was going to die. The Samaritan man would never help him. He had given up hope when he felt a gentle touch. It was the Samaritan man.

"You are hurt," he said. "Lie still and I will help you."

The man could not believe his eyes. The Samaritan man cleaned his wounds and helped him up and then he took him to an inn and paid for him to stay there.'

# The parable of the lost sheep

Sometimes the teachers of the law and the Pharisees would grumble about Jesus, saying, 'Look, he welcomes sinners and he even eats with them.'

In reply to their grumbling Jesus told the next two stories.

'There was once a shepherd who had one hundred sheep. Now this shepherd was responsible for all of his animals and he knew that he had to protect them so, every night he would count them as they went into the sheepfold. When they were all in he knew that they were safe and that no wild animals could attack them.

One night the shepherd was counting his sheep into the sheepfold when he realised that one was missing. He counted them again but still he only got to 99. What should he do? He still had nearly all of his sheep and after all, it was only one that was missing. He knew that it would be dangerous out on the mountainside in the dark. He would have to take great care if he wasn't to get hurt himself.

But he also knew that his little sheep was depending on him and without him it would be in great danger. So he left the 99 in the sheepfold where they were safe and went out into the dark to find the lost sheep. He hunted high and low until finally he heard a little bleating. He had found his sheep. He picked it up and took it home and that night he had a celebration because it was safe.'

# The parable of the prodigal son

The second story that Jesus told was this.

'There was once a man who had two sons. The older son worked for his father but the younger son was restless. One day he asked his father to give him some money so that he could travel and enjoy himself. The father was sad but he loved his son, so he gave him the money and the son left.

At first he had a really good time but soon the money ran out and he began to feel hungry. He didn't want to go home because he was ashamed that he had left his father and not stayed to work for him. He tried to get a job but there was no work in the country he was in, so finally he took a job feeding pigs. By this time he was starving and one day he was so hungry that he wanted to eat the pig food. Suddenly he said to himself, "If I went home, I could tell my father how sorry I am and I could ask him for a job."

So he set off. He was worried about how angry his father might be but he needn't have worried. As he got near his old home his father saw him coming and rushed out to meet him.

"Let's have a party," his father shouted in delight. "I can't believe you've come home. I'm so happy to see you."

That night his older son came in from working in the fields and couldn't believe his eyes. A big party was going on and there was his younger brother who had walked out on them months ago. He felt anger surging inside him. What was his father thinking of?

His father came out to bring him into the party but his son didn't want to come.

"I can't believe you're throwing a big party," he said angrily. "You've not done that for me and I've worked for you for ages."

But his father calmed him down. "Everything I have is for you to share," he said. "You can have a party whenever you want but I thought your younger brother was dead and I've just found out that he isn't. He's come home and that's a great reason to celebrate."'

# Jesus helps his disciples to understand

All through his adult life Jesus taught his disciples about how to live and what to do but as he grew nearer the time when he knew he was going to die, he tried to comfort them and to make them strong for the future.

## My gift to you

He said to them, 'Don't worry or be sad; do not let your hearts be troubled. Trust in God and trust in me. I am going away but I will come back and take you with me so that we will be together. Anyone who loves me will do what I say. The things I have said to you have not come from me but have come from my Father who sent me. I give you peace and the kind of peace I give you is a special peace that nobody else can give. Do not be worried or afraid. This is my gift to you.'

## The Holy Spirit

He talked to them about a new friend they would have in the future, somebody who would help them understand and would make them strong.

'When I go away, I will send a special friend. This friend will be the Holy Spirit, the Spirit of truth that is part of my Father and part of me. Then you will be my witnesses because you have been with me all the time.'

## I am the vine

Jesus told them that they had a special job but that he would help them to do it. 'I am like a vine and you are the branches. If a branch is cut away from the vine, then it will die and will not produce any fruit. You are like that. If you are cut off from me you will find it hard to be good and do good things, so stay with me because God has got a special job for you and he wants you to do wonderful things. This is what I want you to do, love each other as I have loved you. There is no better thing that you can do. I am not going to call you my servants, I call you my friends. You did not choose me, I chose you as my friends and I am asking you to go out and bring joy and love and happiness to the world.'

## You will always have my love with you

Then Jesus said to his friends, 'I have loved you just as my Father loves me. If you do what I have asked, you will always have that love with you. I am telling you this so that you can feel the joy that I feel. I still have a lot of things to tell you but you would not understand them yet. When I go the Spirit of truth will come and be with you and then you will know the truth.'

## Be brave

Jesus knew that his friends would be sad when he left them but he tried to help them understand. 'Now I am going to the person who sent me. I know you are sad because of this but I must tell you the truth. If I do not go, then I cannot send my special friend to you. This friend will help you understand everything and to be brave. I am not alone because the Father is with me. I have told you everything so that you can find peace with me. In the world you will have trouble but be brave for I have conquered the world.'

## Father, protect my friends

Then Jesus prayed to his Father and said, 'Father, protect my friends from evil. Your word is truth. Bless them with the truth. As you sent me into the world, I am sending them. For their sake I bless myself so that they too may be blessed in truth. I want the friends that you have given me to be with me where I am. I have known you and they have known that you sent me. I have told them about you and will carry on doing that so that your love may be in them and I may be in them.'

# The final week

## Jesus enters Jerusalem

Jesus set off with his disciples to go to Jerusalem. As they got nearer to the city they passed through a village. He said to two of his disciples,

'Over there you will find a donkey. Nobody has ever ridden it before. I want you to ask the man who owns it to lend it to you so that I can use it.'

The disciples went off and found the donkey. They asked the man if they could borrow it.

'Our Master needs it,' they said.

The man agreed and the disciples took the donkey back to Jesus. They spread their cloaks on it instead of a saddle and Jesus climbed on.

He rode into the city on the donkey and, as he passed, people recognised him and they began to shout,

'Hurrah for the King; blessed is the King; hosanna to the King.'

And they shouted and cheered as he rode into the city.

But some of the Pharisees and the Jews were not happy and they wanted to get rid of Jesus.

## Jesus drives the merchants from the Temple

Now it was almost time for the Passover so Jesus went to the Temple but, instead of finding a quiet house of prayer, he found lots of people selling oxen and sheep and doves. Money was changing hands and it was like a market. Now Jesus got angry. He made a whip out of cords and he drove all of the merchants and their animals out of the Temple. He knocked over their tables and scattered their money saying, 'Take these things away. Don't make my Father's house into a market!'

The Jews said to him, 'Who are you to do these things? Show us a sign if you are so important!'

And Jesus replied, 'Destroy this Temple and I will build it up again in three days.'

The Jewish people laughed. 'It took 46 years to build this Temple. Are you saying you can do it in three?'

But Jesus was not talking about the Temple he was standing in. He was talking about his own body and how he would raise it up again in three days if the Jews destroyed it.

# Jesus celebrates the Last Supper

It was getting nearer to the Passover and Jesus wanted to celebrate it with his disciples. He told two of them to go and get everything ready.

'Go into the city and you'll see a man carrying a water jug. Follow him and when he goes into a house, ask if we can use the upstairs room for the Passover tonight.'

The disciples did as Jesus asked and that evening they all gathered together to celebrate the Passover.

Before they ate, Jesus took a towel. He wrapped it around his waist and then took a bowl of water and knelt down in front of his disciples to wash their feet, which were dusty and sandy. When he got to Peter, though, Peter was horrified that Jesus should do such a humble task.

'You can't wash my feet,' he said, 'It's not right.'

But Jesus answered, 'If you don't let me do this then you cannot be my friend.'

Then Peter said, 'Then don't just wash my feet, Lord, wash all of me.'

When Jesus had finished he sat down at the table and said to them, 'You call me Master and Lord and that is right. I have done this service for you as an example to show you that it is what I want you to do for each other.'

Then they began their meal. During the meal Jesus took some bread and he blessed it. He broke the bread and then shared it with his disciples.

'Take this and share it. Eat it because this is my body which soon will be given up for you.'

Then he took the cup of wine and he blessed it also. He shared it, passing it around and as he did so he said,

'Take this and share it. Drink it because it is the cup that is my blood which will be poured out for you.'

He looked around at his disciples, friends who had shared so many things with him as he travelled and taught the people and he felt sad because he knew that one of them had turned away from his teachings and soon would betray him and hand him over to the Romans. He looked at the one called Judas because he knew that this was the man.

And Judas got up and left the table.

Then Jesus said to his friends who were left,

'I will only be with you for a little while now because I am going somewhere and this time you can't come with me. So, I am giving you a new commandment today. You must love one another just as I have loved you. It is by this, your love for each other, that everybody will know that you are my disciples.'

Peter was shocked and said, 'Lord, I will never leave you. I will go with you wherever you go.'

But Jesus shook his head sadly. 'Before the cock crows in the morning you will have denied that you know me,' he said.

Peter shook his head in disbelief but Jesus rose from the table. They sang a hymn together and went out to the Mount of Olives.

# Jesus is betrayed

They went to a garden called Gethsemane and Jesus told his disciples to wait and pray for him. Jesus then went a little way off and prayed to his Father. 'If you can,' he prayed, 'please don't let what I am afraid of happen to me.' Then he said sadly, 'But whatever you want, I will do it.'

He went back to his disciples but they had fallen asleep. 'Wake up,' he said. 'Couldn't you stay awake for this little time with me?'

He went back to pray again and again the disciples fell asleep. Finally Jesus prayed a third time and he went back to his disciples and said, 'Get up now because it is time. The Son of Man is going to be betrayed.'

Just as he was speaking, Judas came up with a band of soldiers. Now not all the soldiers knew which one was Jesus so Judas had told them, 'Watch what I do. I will kiss the man who is Jesus then you will know which one he is.'

When they reached Jesus he went straight up to him and kissed him, saying, 'Master.'

The soldiers took hold of Jesus. One of the people who was with him tried to defend him. He took out his sword and cut off the ear of one of the people with Judas but Jesus told him to put his sword away and healed the man's ear. Then they took Jesus away to the high priest.

Most of the disciples were afraid but Peter followed them, keeping a little way behind. When they got to the high priest Peter stood outside and waited by the fire.

The high priest and other important people asked Jesus a lot of questions, trying to trick him into saying that he had broken the law. Outside a girl came up to Peter and spoke to him, 'Aren't you one of that man's friends?' she asked. But Peter was afraid and said hastily, 'No. I'm not one of his followers.'

A little later the girl came back and asked him again, and again he said that he was not a friend of Jesus. Finally, some of the people standing around said, 'Are you sure you're not one of his friends? We're sure we've seen you with him.' Then Peter began to shout loudly and say angrily, 'I tell you, I don't know him.'

The minute he said that he heard a cock crowing and he remembered what Jesus had said. Overcome with sadness he rushed away into the night and wept.

# Jesus is crucified

The next morning Jesus was taken to Pilate who was the Roman in charge of that area. The high priest said that Jesus had committed a crime by saying that he was God and so should be killed. The high priest did not have the power to order that to happen and wanted Pilate to do it.

Pilate asked Jesus questions but he could not find anything that he had done wrong and so he told the priests that but they were not happy.

'He has done wrong,' they said, 'and our law says that he should die.'

So Pilate asked Jesus more questions but still could not find that he had committed a crime. Then he had an idea. It was a special festival time and he knew that the custom was that he could set one prisoner free for the Jews at that special time. Now he knew that there was a man called Barabbas in prison, a wicked man who had killed people. So Pilate went out to the people and said,

'I can set one of these prisoners free – Jesus or Barabbas. Which one do you want me to let go?'

But the people shouted, 'We want you to free Barabbas.'

Pilate asked them, 'So what shall I do with the man you call Jesus?'

And the whole crowd shouted back, 'Crucify him.'

Pilate did not want to upset the crowd but had not found any fault in Jesus so he said to them, 'Why, what has he done wrong?'

But the crowd didn't answer. They just shouted again, 'Crucify him.'

So Pilate, who wanted to please the crowd, gave the order for Jesus to be killed. But first he took a bowl of water and washed his hands in front of the crowd. 'I am doing this to show that it is your will,' he said, 'and I am not guilty of this man's death.'

Then they took Jesus away, and forcing him to carry the cross on which he was to be crucified, they led him to a place called Golgotha where they crucified him with two robbers. Just as Jesus died, he cried out in a loud voice and the whole land became dark.

There was a soldier standing by the cross and he trembled. 'This really was God's son,' he whispered.

Later, some of the friends of Jesus came and took his body down from the cross. They wrapped it in a clean linen cloth and took it to a tomb which belonged to a man called Joseph, and they laid him there. Then they rolled a stone over the entrance.

# What happened next

Pilate had sent a soldier to guard the tomb because the priests were worried that the friends of Jesus would play a trick on people.

'They might steal the body and tell everyone that he rose from the dead,' they said.

So Pilate sent a guard to watch the tomb and sealed up the stone.

Early on the morning of the third day, Mary came to visit the tomb with a friend. On the way they were talking to each other. 'Who will roll the heavy stone away for us to go in?' they said.

But when they got there they could not believe their eyes. The soldier was gone and the great stone had been rolled aside. A young man was sitting there and he was dressed all in white. They were frightened but he said, 'Don't be afraid. You're looking for Jesus, aren't you? Well he has risen and is not here. Go and tell his disciples.'

The two women ran as quickly as they could to tell the disciples and when Peter came to the tomb he found it just as Mary had said.

# Jesus appears to two of the disciples on the road to Emmaus

Later, two of the disciples were travelling along the road on their way to a place called Emmaus. They were talking about what had happened when a man came up to join them.

'What are you talking about?' he asked them.

They were astonished. 'Are you the only person who doesn't know what's happened?' they said. And they told him about what had happened to Jesus and how the two women had found the stone rolled away and an angel had told them that Jesus had risen.

The man listened and walked with them. When they had finished he talked to them about the prophets and the Scriptures and he explained everything to them about the one called Christ. The disciples listened and as they walked, they were overwhelmed with a strange feeling.

Evening drew near and the disciples asked the man to stay with them. He agreed and they sat together. Then he did something very special. He took some bread and blessed it and broke it and, as soon as he did that, the disciples realised that it was Jesus. As soon as they realised this, he vanished.

They were full of excitement. 'Did you feel your heart burning inside you when he spoke to us?' they asked each other. Then they left and hurried back to Jerusalem to tell the others.

# Jesus appears to his disciples

The disciples were gathered together when suddenly Jesus appeared. 'Peace be with you,' he said.

But they were afraid so he said, 'Do not be afraid. I am not a ghost. Look at my hands and feet. Touch me and see that I am real.'

The disciples looked at his hands and feet. There were the wounds from the nails on the cross. They were overwhelmed with joy and amazement. Then Jesus asked for some food and so they gave him some fish and some honeycomb.

Now Thomas was not there when Jesus appeared and when the disciples told him, Thomas did not believe them. Later, when they were all together and the door was shut, Jesus appeared again. He spoke to Thomas. 'Look at my hands and feet,' he said. 'Put your hands into the wounds and see that I am real.'

Thomas was overcome with guilt and answered him, 'My Lord and my God.'

A little while later, Peter and some of the others went fishing at night but they did not catch anything. When the morning came they decided to stop. As they drew nearer to the shore, they saw a person they did not recognise. This man shouted to them, 'Have you caught anything?'

They shouted back, 'No.'

'Drop your net over the right side of your boat and you will find fish.'

They did this and they caught a huge number of fish. As soon as this happened Peter realised that the man on the shore was Jesus and he jumped into the sea to swim to him. The other disciples followed in the boat, dragging the nets with the fish in them.

When they reached the shore they saw a fire and some bread. 'Bring the fish,' said Jesus. They did as he asked and they ate the fish. Then Jesus said to Peter, 'Do you love me?'

'Yes Lord,' said Peter immediately.

Jesus asked him three times and each time Peter promised that he did.

# Jesus goes back to his Father in heaven

Jesus led his disciples out to Bethany. When they got there he blessed them. After he had blessed them he was carried up into heaven and the disciples were filled with joy. They went back to Jerusalem praising God.

# The Acts of the Apostles

# The Early Church

After Jesus had risen from the dead and ascended back to his Father, the apostles tried to live as Jesus wanted and to spread the good news that Jesus had brought.

## The Holy Spirit comes down upon the apostles

After Jesus had gone back to his Father, the apostles went back to Jerusalem and stayed in the upper room. Although they were overjoyed that Jesus had risen, they were also afraid now that he had left them. What if the Jewish people and the Romans did the same thing to them that they had done to Jesus?

They shut all of the doors and windows when, suddenly, a sound like a rushing wind filled the whole room. At the same time, tongues of fire appeared and settled over the head of each one. And each of the apostles was filled with the Holy Spirit.

They suddenly felt brave and strong and they went out into the streets to speak to all of the people. Now, there were many different people in Jerusalem and they all spoke different languages but when the apostles began to speak, they could all understand them.

'What is happening?' they asked each other. 'We don't speak the same language and yet we can all hear what they are saying as if they were speaking in our own tongue.'

Then Peter spoke to everybody.

'Listen,' he said. 'We want to tell you about Jesus, the son of Joseph. He was crucified in this city but now he has risen from the dead. We are the witnesses and we tell you that it is true.'

The people listened in amazement and then asked,

'What should we do?'

'You must be sorry for the things you have done wrong and you must be baptised in the name of Jesus. Then you will receive the gift of the Holy Spirit.'

Three thousand people were baptised that day because of what they saw and heard.

# The apostles are warned not to preach about Jesus

When Jesus had risen from the dead, all of his followers became like a family. Everybody shared everything and nobody was selfish. Nobody wanted anything because they shared all their land and money. They told everybody they knew about Jesus and people respected them.

The priests, though, were not happy. They did not like the things that the disciples were saying and so they had them arrested and thrown into jail. At night, an angel of the Lord opened the prison gates and led them out. 'Go into the Temple,' said the angel, 'and tell the people all about this new life.'

The priests were astonished and angry that they had escaped and sent for them again. 'We told you not to preach,' they said. 'Why are you still doing it?'

The apostles replied, 'We have to obey God before we obey you. We have seen what happened and we need to tell people about it.'

The high priest and the officials were so angry that they wanted to put the apostles to death but a wise Pharisee named Gamaliel persuaded them not to do it. They had the apostles beaten and told them to go but not to preach about Jesus any more. The apostles were happy that they had stood up for the right thing and suffered in the name of Jesus.

# Other people attack the disciples

There were many other people who did not like the disciples telling everybody about Jesus. They wanted the disciples to stop and so they started to attack them. One of these people was named Saul. He went around arresting people and sending them to prison if they spoke about Jesus. It did not stop the disciples though. They carried on telling people about Jesus.

# God speaks to Saul

Saul was still looking for Christians and attacking them. He was one of their worst enemies until one day, a very strange thing happened. He was on his way to Damascus, riding down the road on his horse when suddenly, out of nowhere, a light shone all around him. His horse reared and he fell off onto the ground. He heard a voice saying, 'Saul, why are you attacking me?' He was afraid and he asked, 'Who are you?' The voice replied, 'I am Jesus and you are attacking me.'

Saul was astonished and frightened. He lay there, trembling and asked, 'What do you want me to do?'

The voice said to him, 'Get up and go into the city. When you get there you will be told what to do.' The men with him could hear the voice and were astonished because nobody else was there. Saul stood up but he realised that he could not see anything. He was blind, so the people who were with him led him into Damascus.

In the city was a holy man called Ananias. Jesus spoke to him in a vision.

'I want you to go and pray over a man called Saul,' he said.

'Lord,' answered Ananias, 'I have heard of this man. He is attacking your followers and is pleased when he arrests them.'

'I want you to go,' said Jesus, 'because I have chosen him to spread my message.'

So, when Saul was led into the city, the holy man went to find him and prayed over him. When he had prayed, Saul suddenly realised that he could see again. He knew that God had given him a special mission. From that moment he stopped attacking the Christians. He went to stay with the disciples at Damascus and became one himself. He started to tell everybody about Jesus and he changed his name to Paul.

People who heard him were amazed. 'Wasn't this the man who was always attacking the followers of Jesus?' they said. 'Now he's preaching about him.'

But Paul continued to follow Jesus and to spread his message of love and forgiveness.

# The church leaders send letters to the new followers of Jesus

As the news about Jesus spread, more and more people wanted to follow him. These people lived in different places and so the Church leaders wrote letters to them to encourage them and to teach them.

## St Paul writes to the Romans

*Greetings.*
> Grace to you and peace from God our Father and the Lord Jesus Christ.
> Let me tell you some things that God wants.

### Don't judge others

You need to know that no matter who you are, there is no excuse for judging other people. If you judge others, then you are condemning yourself. God has no favourites.

### The Holy Spirit will help you

The Holy Spirit comes to help us when we are not strong. When we cannot choose words to pray properly, the Spirit will help us by taking our prayer to God and God who knows everything in our hearts, will know perfectly well what we mean.

With God on our side who can be against us? Nothing can come between us and the love of God. Even when we are worried or troubled, nothing can come between us and Jesus who brings us God's love.

### God gives us all different gifts

God never takes back his gifts. How rich are the depths of God; God's wisdom and knowledge are deep. Everything that exists comes from God. Let us praise God forever.

All of us, together with Jesus, make up one body and because we are all parts of this body, we belong to each other. Our gifts are all different but what we must all do is use our gifts and not waste them. Treat everybody the same and try to really care for others. Do not give up when things get difficult. Always be hopeful because this makes you cheerful.

### Remember the most important commandment

The most important commandment is that you should love one another. You must love your neighbour as yourself. Love is the one thing that cannot hurt your neighbour; that is why it is the answer to everything.

# St Paul writes to the Corinthians

*Greetings.*

I never stop thanking God for all the gifts and graces you have received through Jesus. I thank him that you have been made so rich in so many ways.

## This is how to follow God

We prove that we follow God by being true, by being patient and by being kind. We should show that we have a spirit of holiness and that we give love without showing off.

Do not forget that if you only give a little, you will only receive a little; the more you give, the more you will receive. Everyone should give cheerfully because God loves cheerful givers. There is no limit to the blessings that God will send you.

## We are all important

A human body is made up of many different parts. All of these parts have their own job but together they make one body. It is the same with Jesus. We are all baptised with the Holy Spirit and although we are all different and have different gifts and jobs, we make up the body of Christ.

## Love is more important than anything

If I am really good at lots of things but do not have love within me then I am nothing. Love is patient and kind. It is not jealous and it does not show off. It is not rude or selfish and it does not take offence. Instead, love delights in the truth and is always ready to forgive and to hope.

# St Paul writes to the Galatians

*Greetings.*

## I have been chosen to spread the Word

God, who had specially chosen me before I was born, called me through his grace and chose me to tell people about the good news of love and forgiveness.

When I went to Jerusalem I went to see the leading men and I told them about the way that I was telling people the good news. I did this because I was worried that they would not approve of the way that I was spreading the message of Jesus but they said that they could see that I had been chosen to spread the Word in my own way.

## Be led by the Holy Spirit

If you are led by the Spirit, people will not find things wrong with you. What the Spirit brings is love, joy, peace, patience, kindness, goodness, trustfulness, gentleness and self-control.

# St Paul writes to the Ephesians

*Greetings.*

## God chose us

Before the world was made, God chose us to be holy and to live through love in his presence. He wanted us to be his children. He has showered us with the richest grace.

It is through Jesus that God claimed us as his own. We were chosen from the very beginning to be the people who put their hope in Jesus. Now you have heard the message of truth and the good news of love and you have been given the gift of the Holy Spirit.

## God brings peace and forgiveness

God loves us with so much love that he is generous with his forgiveness. He has brought us to life with Jesus and has saved us through his gift of grace. We are God's work of art.

Jesus came to bring the good news of peace, peace to everybody who is far away and peace to everybody who is close by. Through Jesus, everybody has a way to come to God our Father.

## This is how we should treat each other

Put up with each other kindly. Try not to think of yourself all the time but be gentle and patient with other people. Do everything you can to keep the peace between you so that you are a team, united by God's Holy Spirit.

Be friends with each other. Be kind, forgiving each other the way that God forgives you. Try to be like God because you are children of God and God loves you. Follow Jesus by loving the way that he loves you. You were in darkness once but now you are full of God's light. Be like children of light.

Children, be obedient to your parents – that is your duty. This is one of the commandments – that you should honour your parents. Parents, you should guide your children as God does.

# St Paul writes to the Philippians

*Greetings.*

## Jesus was raised high

Jesus was divine but he did not cling to this. He became a man and he accepted death. But God raised him high and gave him a name which is above all other names.

## You will shine like bright stars

My dear friends, do all you have to do without complaining or arguing and then you will be innocent and genuine, perfect children of God. You will shine in the world like bright stars because you are offering it the word of life.

## Stay faithful to God

My brothers and sisters, try to follow my rule. Copy everybody who is already doing the right thing. Do not give in to bad things but stay faithful to God.

# St Paul writes to the Colossians

*Greetings.*

## You are God's chosen people

You are God's chosen people. God loves you and God calls each of you as a special person, so you must try to always be caring, kind and gentle. Be careful how you treat others; don't show off and always be patient with them. Forgive each other straight away but most of all, love each other. And may the peace of God live in your hearts.

# A letter from the church leaders to the Hebrews

*Greetings.*

## God tells us what to do through Jesus

God has spoken to us through his Son, Jesus. Jesus is the shining light that shows us God's glory.

Every day you should keep encouraging each other, so that none of you get tempted to do the wrong thing.

God will not forget all you have done, the love you have for him or the services you have done for other people. Our hope is that you will always go on showing the same sincerity.

## God promises the Holy Spirit

God said, 'Soon I will make a new promise. I will put my law into the minds of my people; I will write it in their hearts. I will be their God and they will be my people.'

The Holy Spirit tells us that this is what God has promised. 'I will put my laws into their hearts and write them on their minds. I will never think about their mistakes.'

## This is how to live

Let us be truthful in heart and filled with faith. Let our minds be clear and not have any feeling of having done something wrong. Let us always hope. Let us be concerned for each other, acting with love and doing good things.

Always be wanting peace and to be holy. Be careful that nobody cuts themselves off from God's grace. Don't let bitter and mean feelings grow among you and make trouble because this can spoil a whole community.

Continue to love each other like brothers and sisters and try to always make newcomers welcome. Try not to be greedy and to be content with what you have got. Remember that God has said that he will not let us down.

# St James writes to the people of God

*Greetings.*

## God will help us

My brothers and sisters, there will always be things in life that are difficult but, when they come, try to see the best in them. If you need understanding then ask God and he will give it without grudge.

Everything that is perfect comes from the Father of all light. By his own choice he has made us his children by giving us the message of truth.

## You must show your love in your actions

Sometimes people say that they believe in God but they never do a single thing to help anyone else. Is this really believing in God? You must not just tell them that you believe but you must show them by doing good and kind things for others.

If you are a wise and clever person, you show it by your good life. If there is jealousy, then people fall out and fight. God gives us a wisdom that is pure and helps us make peace. It is always kind and caring.

# St Peter writes to the people of God

*Greetings.*

## Let your love be real; you are the people of God

You have faith in God through Jesus. The good news that has been brought to you by Jesus will last forever. Let your love for each other be real and from the heart.

You are a chosen race. You are a royal priesthood, a holy people. You are a people chosen specially to sing the praise of God who has called you out of darkness and into his wonderful light. You are the people of God.

Each one of you has been given a special gift. You are responsible for these gifts from God and must use them to help others.

## You must play your part

I hope that you will have more and more grace and peace as you know Jesus better. Jesus has given us many things but we need to do our part as well. We need to be kind and caring, to be loving and patient. We need to have self-control.

# St John writes to the people of God

*Greetings.*

## We must live a life of love

My children, our love is not to be just words or talk, but it has to be something real and active. This is the only way we can be sure that we are children of the truth.

God has asked us to keep his commandments and live the kind of life he wants. His commandments are these: that we believe in Jesus and that we love one another as he told us to.

So, my dear people, let us love one another since love comes from God and everyone who loves, knows God because God is love. God showed his love when he sent his Son, Jesus, into the world so that we could have a better life. This is how great God's love is for us.

Since God has loved us so much, we too should love each other. No one has ever seen God but as long as we love each other, God will live in us and his love will be complete.

This is what the truth is. God has given us eternal life and this life is in his Son, Jesus. Anyone who has Jesus has life.

If you want to love then you must follow the rules that Jesus gave us. The most important rule that you have heard is that you must live a life of love.